Dear Reader

Also by Cathy Rentzenbrink

A Manual for Heartache
The Last Act of Love

CATHY RENTZENBRINK

Dear Reader

The Comfort and Joy
of Books

PICADOR

First published 2020 by Picador
an imprint of Pan Macmillan
The Smithson, 6 Briset Street, London EC1M 5NR
Associated companies throughout the world
www.panmacmillan.com

ISBN 978-1-5098-9152-8

1 3 5 7 9 8 6 4 2

A CIP catalogue record for this book is available from the British Library.

Typeset in Warnock by Jouve (UK), Milton Keynes
Printed and bound by CPI Group (UK) Ltd, Croydon, CR0 4YY

Visit **www.picador.com** to read more about all our books
and to buy them. You will also find features, author interviews and
news of any author events, and you can sign up for e-newsletters
so that you're always first to hear about our new releases.

For Matthew Jan Rentzenbrink
A book of your own

'We've got to live, no matter how many skies have fallen.'

D. H. Lawrence, *Lady Chatterley's Lover*

'My mission in life is not merely to survive, but to thrive; and to do so with some passion, some compassion, some humour, and some style.'

Maya Angelou

Dear Reader

I'm lying on the floor of my new house in Cornwall surrounded by boxes. I'm supposed to be unpacking, but my back hurts and I've remembered some advice I was once given: to lie flat on the floor with my knees bent and to put a book under my head. The book is a big blue hardback that contains all four of Daphne du Maurier's Cornish novels. *Rebecca* is my favourite. I think about the story; the timid girl whose name we never get to know, who is working as a companion to a demanding woman in the South of France when she meets and marries newly widowed Max de Winter. He is twice her age and breathes experience and wealth. She goes back with him to Manderley, his beautiful house by the sea, where she walks among the azaleas in her garden and frets about how inadequate she is compared to Max's dead wife Rebecca. Like me, the girl is a bit of a scruff. She worries about not having the right clothes and that her hair is a mess. We also have nail-biting in common. I hold my hands up and look at them. The skin around both my thumbs is red raw.

How many times have I read *Rebecca*? Ten, twenty? I don't remember the first time but I will have been younger than the girl then, and now I am older than Max de Winter himself. I am feeling my years today; tired and worn out from the stress of moving. It is the right thing, to come back to Cornwall, to be close to my parents. I feel the lure of nature, the desire to exchange sitting in traffic for walking by the sea. I want to have a garden and spend time cultivating it.

But so far all I've done in between emptying boxes is stare at my phone, watching the ongoing soap opera of politics. If I were reading a novel, I might find it enjoyable, though unrealistic. It would be funny, if it were a satire. It does me no good, I know, to be too close to this absurdity, to be continually confronted with evidence of the folly and vanity of my fellow humans. I need to find a way through, to stop spinning myself out over things I can't control.

And as I lie there, surrounded by boxes, looking up at the half-filled shelves, at the books that have followed me from place to place, I find my answer. I will be my own doctor and prescribe the best medicine: a course of rereading. I will make piles of my most treasured books and read through them, taking comfort not only in each book itself but also in the reassuring knowledge that there are many more to come. Something shifts in my body. I feel better already, just at the thought of turning off my phone and spending my evenings curled up with a good book. This is what I have always done. When the bite of real life is too brutal, I retreat into made-up worlds and tread well-worn paths. I don't crave the new when I feel like this, but look for solace in the familiar. It is as though in re-encountering my most-loved fictional characters, I can also reconnect with my previous selves and come out feeling less fragmented. Reading built me and always has the power to put me back together again.

I roll over to one side and pull myself up. Where shall I begin? I pick up the big blue hardback as I mull over my options. I feel *Rebecca* call to me with the promise of glamour and mystery, but then a slim volume on the top shelf catches my eye.

My initial attempts at shelving have been chronological; I've been organizing my books according to the age I was when I first read them. I'll do that. I'll start at the very beginning. I reach up and my journey begins.

Dreaming of Narnia

Last night I dreamt I went to Narnia again. I stood under the lamppost, felt the snow crunch under my feet, and shivered despite the warmth of my fur coat. I didn't know if I had arrived in happy or dark times. Was this an ordinary winter or the endless reign of the White Witch? Would I be brave enough for the challenges ahead? Or would I succumb to the lure of enchanted Turkish delight? I don't know what age I was in the dream, if I was the woman I am now or the girl who stepped into the wardrobe when she was a child. I've been dreaming of Narnia almost all my life.

Where did it begin? Reading has always been a great source of comfort, knowledge, pleasure and joy. It is the most central aspect of my identity; the truest thing I could say about myself is, 'I am a reader.' Growing up, I often preferred reading to engaging with real life. Lost and sad in my late twenties, I found consolation when I

4

got a job in a bookshop. When I briefly dallied with internet dating I described myself as 'Amiable Bookworm'. Pregnant with my son, Matt, I patted my bump and dreamed of the books we would read together. The first thing I do in any new place is look for the bookshop and the library. When I make a friend, I wonder what sits on their shelves.

My granny gave me my first book when I was a few months old. The pages were made of cloth and it was about the seaside. My mother tells me I used to gum on it for hours, staring at the letters as though I knew that words were going to be important to me. I was alert around books; Mum couldn't read me to sleep, because I would get increasingly excited as the story went on. Reading woke me up rather than calmed me down.

I don't remember learning to read. It feels like something that happened by magic rather than a skill that I had to acquire. 'What shall I do with this little girl?' asked my fairy godmother as she leaned over my carrycot. 'I know! I will make her a reader.' And so she waved her wand and sealed my fate, and gave me a gift that has brightened my days, expanded my horizons, and kept me company through the darkest hours.

The first stories I remember were not in books but sung to me by my dad. He was an orphan who had run away to sea from Ireland when he was fifteen. He met my mother when his ship docked into Falmouth three years later. They looked at each other across Custom House Quay and that was that. Four years later I arrived, and then my brother, Matty. Dad took work on dry land so we could be together, and we lived in a caravan so we could follow him around the country as he did various dirty jobs that involved construction and drilling. It was a time before seatbelts and radios in cars, so Matty and I roamed free and unbuckled on the back seat of the Land Rover as Dad sang about brave Irish rebels and wanderers. The men in the songs were always on the move, often working hard and being betrayed by women. Sometimes they were fighting for Ireland and being badly treated by the British. I used to beg for more and loved to sing along.

When we were nearing school age, Dad became a tin miner so we could stay in the same place. We went back to Cornwall and lived in a bungalow in Lanner at the top of a hill. Mum was doing an Open University degree. She'd tell Matty and I that if we let her study for an hour she would read us a chapter of *The Lion, the Witch and the Wardrobe*. The time passed so slowly as we waited to be transported to Narnia.

Once there were four children called Peter, Susan, Edmund and Lucy who are evacuated from London during the Blitz, to live with an old professor in a mysterious house that has secrets even he knows nothing about. One rainy day, exploring, Lucy peers into a big wardrobe full of fur coats. She walks in. There's another rail of coats. This wardrobe is enormous, she thinks, as something crunches under her feet. Mothballs? No, it's snow! There are trees and a lamppost. Lucy meets a faun called Mr Tumnus who has the legs of a goat but is shaped like a man from the waist up. When Lucy explains how she got there, Mr Tumnus thinks she has come from the bright city of War Drobe in the far land of Spare Oom, and says that if he had only worked harder at geography when he was a little faun he would know about those strange countries. Lucy has found her way to Narnia, and so begin the adventures that will see her, Peter, Susan and Edmund join Aslan the lion to triumph over the White Witch and bring spring and happiness back to these frozen lands.

The Lion, the Witch and the Wardrobe was published in 1950, and the descriptions of food take on an added lustre when you think of them against the backdrop of post-war austerity. Mr Tumnus gives Lucy a brown boiled egg for tea, and sardines on toast, and then a sugar-topped cake. When Lucy returns to Narnia with the other children, Mr Beaver fries up fish and potatoes and Mrs Beaver tops it off with a gloriously sticky marmalade roll. Sweet rationing didn't come to an end until

1953. Who wouldn't do almost anything for unlimited Turkish delight and a warm foamy drink served from a jewelled cup?

My early memories are flashes, dreamlike in the way they start and stop with little logic. They tend to involve either reading or shame, and sometimes both. At my first school in Lanner I had a kind teacher who rejoiced in how well I could read and write. She sent me up to read to the teacher in the class above and it was too much; not the teacher but the other, bigger children watching me. I looked down and saw my wee running between the cracks of the floorboards. This is the image I can still see in my mind. I went home with my wet knickers in a carrier bag wearing a spare pair from a box in the school office. My mum washed them and made me take them back in, which was almost as shaming as having wet myself in the first place. Every day I'd bring them back home again and pretend I'd forgotten to hand them over.

When the tin mines shut down, we moved from Cornwall to Yorkshire so that Dad could take a job sinking shafts on Selby coalfield. He worked at a place called Stillingfleet and could never quite wash the coal dust out of his eyes, so he always looked as though he was wearing mascara.

I was five and excited at the prospect of new friends, but the children at school teased me for having a posh voice, which must have been how my half-Irish, half-Cornish accent sounded to them. I was used to being petted and admired for my reading but my new teacher, Mrs C, didn't believe I could have read the books I said I had, and made me start the reading scheme again from the beginning. This wouldn't have mattered as I liked rereading, but she wouldn't let me skip through them so I was stuck looking at the same pages with big letters and pictures. I'd get bored and look out of the window, and then she'd tell me off for not paying attention. I was in continual fear of bringing her wrath down upon me for putting the colouring pencils back in the wrong place or spilling drops of paint on the floor or not being able to choke down my milk, which had been left to stand in the sun all morning.

Mrs C had white curly hair that looked like balls of cotton wool. She had enormous nostrils that I'd try not to look up when she loomed over me. She liked to say that 'askers don't get'.

One day a child had an enormous bag of pineapple cubes, smuggled into school by an older sibling and handed over at playtime. I longed for one. I loved boiled sweets. We bought them in quarters from the village shop. They would last for ages if you sucked them but I was a bit of a cruncher. I'd had pear drops and cola cubes but never pineapple before. Askers don't get, I thought.

I watched the clamour as the bag holder enjoyed their time in the sun and eked out deciding who to favour. I hung around hopefully, trying to hide my desperation. I could almost feel the texture on my tongue. Then, the bag was empty. The crowds dispersed. I was unsatisfied, uncubed, unloved. It isn't true, I thought, that askers don't get, though I remain pretty incapable of putting myself forward in any way. I would still rather not have a pineapple cube than suffer the indignity of asking and being refused.

When I moved up a year the teacher, Mrs F, was less cross, though still keen on putting me in my place. We had periods of free reading and there was a series I loved about buccaneers. I tore through one and went to the trolley to get another. 'Sit back down,' ordered Mrs F, 'you can't possibly have finished that book already.' Everyone stared and laughed.

I read abridged versions of *Great Expectations* and *A Tale of Two Cities* from that trolley. I didn't know they were abridged, and it was a surprise a few years later to realize how long and dull most of Dickens is. I've never quite got over it or been able to recapture that burst of excitement I felt for Dickens on our first acquaintance.

I wasn't good at everything by any means. My handwriting wasn't neat compared to the other girls, and I had no finesse with art or crafting and would end up with splodges over my pictures. Sums were tricky. We played this hideous game called Fizz Buzz which was about multiples of fives and threes. Everyone started off standing up but you had to sit down when you made a mistake, which I always did straight away. I didn't know my left from right and wasn't great at telling the time, so I never worked out why my teachers were so aggravated about my reading and the long words: 'What happened to you, did you swallow a dictionary?' they'd say. Why were they so unkind? They didn't like incomers, I suppose, and were even more unpleasant to the two gypsy children and the one mixed-race girl in our class.

One day Dad went into the Foresters Arms – one of Carlton's three pubs. He was drinking at the bar when he heard two men discussing our family. 'I've heard the wife is educated,' one of them said, 'but the husband is a rough bugger.'

When Dad told us about it later, Mum was cross on his behalf but he just laughed. 'Don't you worry about me,' he said, 'I'm used to it. Anyway, they've got us about right.' We later found out that one of the men was Mrs C's husband.

Dad was having to acquire a little bit of education himself. He'd stopped going to school after his mother died and had always managed to duck and dive around his inability to read and write by getting friends to fill in forms for him and pretending to have forgotten his glasses if he had to go into a bank. Now, a new law meant he needed to be able to complete shift reports, so he signed up for evening classes in Selby. He could only go two out of every three weeks because of his shift pattern, and he told the tutor that he just needed to be able to write in sentences. The other students were all kids who had failed their O levels and called him Grandad. At home we had a big red book full of spellings; Mum would test us both together and I would always win. Dad couldn't understand how it came so easily to me and thought I was a genius.

There wasn't a bookshop for miles, but we went into Selby every Friday night to go to the supermarket, and I was allowed to choose a book in return for being cooperative and helpful. I loved Enid Blyton: *The Magic Faraway Tree*, *The Five Find-Outers and Dog*, *The Secret Seven* and *The Famous Five*. There was also the library in Snaith, the next village along. Grown-up books were on the ground floor and the whole of the upstairs was for children. We went a couple of times a week, which was a great delight for me and a bit of a chore for Matty. We were allowed six books each and I always agonized over my choices, unable to narrow down the big pile of everything I wanted. Matty would only get out one or two – and only then because Mum encouraged him – and would let me use up the rest of his allocation. Once we got home, I'd rattle through them at top speed and not want to do anything else. I liked having several books on the go at any time and would leave them in every room and hung over the edge of the bath. 'I'll throw them away if you don't tidy them up,' Mum would shout. So unreasonable, I thought.

Bad weather weekends were a treat. Mum would always say it was a shame that we couldn't go out for fresh air but I revelled in staying in, tucked up in a corner with a book. Any ordinary rainy afternoon could be transformed by the act of reading.

I'm pretty sure that as soon as I knew what a book was, I wanted to write one myself. From very early on, when asked what I wanted to do when I grew up, I would say I wanted to be a detective or an author. No one ever took me seriously. 'You can't do that,' I was repeatedly told. 'Maybe, if you work very hard, you can work in a building society or possibly even become a teacher.' I still wanted to be an author. But then I also wanted to climb a magic tree, or solve mysteries with a gang of child detectives, sleep on an island on my own, and find a wardrobe that would take me to another world. Maybe being a writer was equally impossible, exotic and out of reach.

Most people apart from my parents told me what I wasn't allowed to do. Books, on the other hand, urged me on. There were no limits.

Over the years, I have lost count of the people who have told me that Narnia was their way into independent reading. Perhaps this is because *The Lion, the Witch and the Wardrobe* is not only a cracking story in its own right, but also represents the way every book offers an invitation to open a door and find a way to another world. It is both simple and profound to consider the vastness of human experience that sits on one small shelf of books.

I hope I'll keep revisiting Narnia in my dreams. It always feels like a privilege that I shouldn't take for granted. Perhaps, as happens with the Pevensie children, one day I will be too old. But I will always have Narnia in my heart. Maybe I should take the professor's advice: 'Don't go trying to use the same route twice. Indeed, don't try to get there at all. It'll happen when you're not looking for it.' Let's hope he's right.

Children's Books I Love to Reread

My childhood favourites remind me of a time without responsibility when I still believed in happy endings. I feel powerfully connected to my son, Matt, when we share something that I read as a girl. The years fall away and we are just two children allowing our imaginations to be set free.

The Wind in the Willows by Kenneth Grahame
The story of Toad, Mole and Ratty started off in letters that Grahame wrote to his son from his motoring holiday in Cornwall. He sent this from the Greenbank Hotel in Falmouth: 'Have you heard about the Toad? He was never taken prisoner by brigands at all. It was all a horrid low trick of his. He wrote that letter himself – the letter saying that a hundred pounds must be put in the hollow tree. And he got out of the window early one morning, and went off to a town called Buggleton and went to the Red Lion Hotel and there he found a party that had just motored down from London, and while they were having breakfast he went into the stable-yard and found their motor-car and went off in it without even saying

Poop-poop! And now he has vanished and everyone is looking for him, including the police. I fear he is a bad low animal.'

Jennings Goes to School by Anthony Buckeridge
The author of these boarding school stories was a teacher and is gifted at putting small boys on the page in all their boisterous and unwise glory. I laugh my head off at the antics of Jennings and Darbishire, and the old-fashioned language is part of the fun. One of our house rules is that Matt is allowed to insult me as long as he is quoting from a book. I prefer 'record stinker' from *The Voyage of the Dawn Treader* over 'hairy ruin' from *Jennings*, but a rule is a rule.

Biggles Learns to Fly by Captain W. E. Johns
I first read these tales of fighter pilots when I was much younger than the men in their flying machines, but now Biggles and his friends seem like boys to me, which they were. The books are a bit dated now, but they are good adventure stories and encourage a discussion about the futility of war. They also aid gratitude in daily life. We went through a stage of saying, 'Don't grouse, we're lucky to be alive' to each other, as Biggles's navigator Mark says to him when they have to swim around barbed wire after crash landing on the wrong side of the lines.

The Railway Children by Edith Nesbit

'Girls are just as clever as boys, and don't you forget it,' says the father of Bobbie, Peter and Phyllis just before he is taken away from them. This gently heroic tale of how a mother copes when her husband is wrongfully arrested is the more powerful for being seen through the eyes of her perceptive daughter, Bobbie, who is clever, kind and never gives up. I am unable to read this slim book without crying at least six times, usually in all the same places.

Little Women by Louisa May Alcott

I can't remember a time when the March sisters – Meg, Jo, Beth and Amy – were not a part of my life. I most identify with Jo, and her tomboyish ways. I was always happier playing with boys than girls when I was younger and liked to scribble, as Jo does. I still reread *Little Women* often, especially at Christmas as it offers an antidote to the excesses of festive consumption. It makes me cry, but I finish it feeling glad and grateful to be safe and warm, with no one I love being away at war or catching scarlet fever.

Girls in Books

I was eight years old when I learnt that books have the power to help in difficult times. We had moved to Scotland for a few months because Dad was offered a job at a big mine called Castlebridge. School was huge and terrifying, and I didn't always understand the teachers. Once, Mrs P made me stand on a chair because I didn't know what nine times seven came to. As I stood up there, red-faced and tearful in front of everyone, it was a tiny consolation to remember that Amy in *Little Women* had been similarly shamed when her teacher caught her with a contraband bag of pickled limes.

When we moved up a year, there was a humiliating system of seat distribution where we had to write down who we wanted to sit with. No one picked me, so I ended up on a table with the other unpopular kids, one of whom continually dripped with snot. If I were a character in a novel, I would have found kindred spirts among them, but I didn't. We just sat there, sullen and miserable. Somehow, I had gone from being too clever for my own good to not being clever at all.

It was hard having no friends at school, but I devoured stories of girls in books. I loved Enid Blyton's boarding school stories, *Malory Towers* and *St Clare's*. I wanted to play lacrosse and eat midnight feasts – ginger cake! Sardines! – and be the sort of person who stuck up for others. I'm not sure I fully twigged that boarding schools existed out in the real world – I wanted to go to one in the same way I wanted to visit Narnia.

I was also keen on the *Chalet School* books set in the Alps, where everyone had to speak lots of languages. There was *What Katy Did* and *What Katy Did at School* and *The Abbey Girls*, and *Flambards* by K. M. Peyton. They showed girls facing moral dilemmas, and I liked to imagine how I would behave in a similar situation and hope I would do the right thing.

Mum bought Matty the *Beano* every week because it was the only printed matter he would voluntarily engage with. She read to him every day and I'd listen along to *Fungus the Bogeyman* and *Stig of the Dump*, often while still reading my own book. What Matty really liked was to be outside playing football. He had plenty of pals, so I'd hang around with them if Mum chased me outside in her continual quest that I consume fresh air.

I was a compliant and obedient child, but I would disobey my parents when it came to bedtime and the lure of my latest book was too great to ignore. The girls in the school stories read after lights out by using a torch under the covers. I didn't have a torch, but in the summer the daylight stretched way past my bedtime, and I pioneered a method of standing next to my window with my head the other side of the curtain so I could carry on reading. I had to listen for the sound of the stairs so I could scarper back across the room and be under the covers when Mum came up to check on us. One night the story was so engrossing that I forgot to keep an ear out and got caught. Mum told me off for being deceitful. I hadn't thought of it like that and was mortified. At home, as in books, the worst sin was to be sneaky and tell lies. From then on I lay awake bookless, staring at the ceiling and thinking up plots full of boarding schools, twins and orphans.

One morning Matty woke me up by bouncing on my bed, shouting, 'Grandad's dead and we're off to Cornwall for the funeral.'

Mum was in the bath crying. 'It's so funny,' she said. 'Yesterday I was so worried about the Falklands War, and now I wonder why I didn't spend the whole day feeling glad that Dad was alive.' I was sad that Mum was sad, but like Matty I did find it a bit exciting, and it was wonderful to get a few days off school. I only fully realized that my lovely grandad was no longer alive when I saw the coffin on the morning of the funeral.

When the rest of my family went back to Scotland, I stayed with Granny to keep her company. In the front room was a dresser that Grandad had made, housing a jingle jar to save money for cancer research and a shelf of battered Agatha Christies Granny had bought from church fetes. For each one I read, she put ten pence in the jingle jar. I had finished them all by the end of the week.

We only stayed in Scotland a few months. One of the men on Dad's shift committed a robbery and used work as an alibi, saying he had been underground at the time. Dad refused to back him up and the police wanted him to be a witness at the trial. Shortly after that, the man and his brothers cornered Dad in a cabin on site and threatened him. Another man warned Dad to get his wife and children away, and one day when we came home from school Mum said we were leaving that night to go to stay with Granny.

I remember how nervous Mum was, waiting for Dad to ring every night. A few days later, Dad said he was sick of not being supported by the big bosses at the mine and he'd managed to get an immediate start at Maltby pit. It turned out to be a blessing that our house in Yorkshire hadn't sold, and we happily moved back in. I was thrilled to be reunited with my friends and my old school now seemed small and friendly.

With hindsight, I'm surprised how much I knew about what was going on, but my parents had a great way of telling us a version of the truth we could cope with, so we weren't in the dark but still felt protected. It did feel a bit like something out of Enid Blyton, and I was impressed with Dad for standing up for the truth and refusing to be intimidated by bullies. I loved my dad with a huge passion. He was jolly and kind, different from most of my friends' fathers who – like Enid Blyton's Uncle Quentin – were grumpy and didn't enjoy being around noisy children. I was also fascinated by his story, and would get him to tell me again and again about when his mother died and how he stopped going to school. He seemed more like a fictional character than anyone else I knew, this orphan boy who had run away to sea when he was not much bigger than me.

Perhaps this love for my orphan father was why I fell so enduringly in love with Anne Shirley from *Anne of Green Gables* by L. M. Montgomery. Anne's parents died of a fever when she was three months old, and she was passed around various families for years, before ending up in an asylum. Her dreams come true when she is sent to stay with Matthew and Marilla Cuthbert at Green Gables and they decide to keep her, even though she is not the boy they asked for. They teach her to say her prayers and send her to school, and Anne turns out to be a blessing.

The Anne books are gentle social comedies and I like the details of daily life and domestic history. When Marilla goes out to a meeting of the Aid Society, Anne is allowed to invite her best friend Diana to tea, though not to use the rosebud spray tea set which is reserved for visits from the minister. Marilla says they can finish up the raspberry cordial left over from the church social, but Anne gets the bottles mixed up and 'sets Diana drunk' by serving her three glasses of Marilla's currant wine. Diana's mother refuses to let them play together after that and Anne is heartbroken, but when Diana's little sister has croup on a night all the adults are at a political meeting, Anne saves her life with a bottle of ipecac and is then invited to tea, where Mrs Barry gets out the very best china set and offers fruit cake, pound cake, doughnuts and two types of preserves, just as if, Anne tells Marilla later, Anne is proper company. Anne is now an honoured guest in the Barry house but continues to get into scrapes elsewhere.

Anne and I had much in common. I had ginger hair, like her, and we were both chatterboxes and bookworms who were teased for our use of long words. Anne and her school friends form a story club and adopt pseudonyms. Anne's nom de plume is Rosamond Montmorency. Ruby Gillis puts too much lovemaking into her stories, Jane Andrews's tales are always too sensible, and Diana kills her characters off because she can't think what else to do with them. I was always trying to inveigle my friends into writing stories with me, with limited success. Anne eventually becomes a writer, and there are bits about rejection and ambition that I loved as a girl and continue to resonate now I'm a writer myself.

The books are also excellent on the pleasures of reading. Anne gets into trouble for reading *Ben-Hur* when she should be studying Canadian history, but she just can't stop until she knows how the chariot race turns out. This is exactly how I still feel about a good book. Once lured in and involved with the characters, I find it painful to stop. The way Anne gets Matthew to lock up a tempting book in the jam closet until she's done her homework reminds me of how I've always struggled to work in libraries, because I can hear the books I haven't read clamouring for my attention and I usually allow myself to be led astray.

I shared a problem with Anne, one she identified on her thirteenth birthday: 'My besetting sin is imagining too much and forgetting my duties.' I was often in trouble for having wandered off from a task, and twice I set our house on fire because I got engrossed in a book and forgot what I was doing. Once I was cooking potato waffles and the grill pan caught alight. The other time we'd been sent home from school because of the snow, and I wanted to go out to play again but was soaked. I decided to dry out my wet wellies by propping them up on a footstool and balancing them on the grate of our coal fire. (No, I don't know why I thought that was a good idea, either.) I went upstairs to change out of my sodden uniform and I picked up a book. I can't remember what it was, but it's tempting to think I was reading about Anne getting distracted by reading at the precise moment that black smoke started billowing up the stairs. I ran down to the kitchen and opened the cupboards, looking for a container. I found an old Quality Street tin, filled it from the tap, and had to run between fire and tap several times before it was out. Then I had a good cry and rang Mum at work to confess. I spent that weekend scrubbing soot off the ceiling.

I loved Anne herself – my kindred spirit – but I also enjoyed the conversation between the women; the gossip about who might marry who and why people behaved in the way that they did. The books are notable for what doesn't happen. There's no hint of menstruation or sex, and babies are 'secret dreams' or 'tender hopes', delivered by the stork. This was so different from real life, where we were herded into a classroom at school to be taught about periods, after which all the boys ran up to us and shouted, 'Have you started yet?' Gilbert Blythe wouldn't do *that*, I thought.

Orphans in Books

Being orphaned often opens the door to adventure in books, as children are left to fend for themselves without a parent making them do homework or go to bed on time. This was probably the first time I noticed the disconnect between fiction and real life – that in real life being orphaned was emphatically *not* a good thing.

Great Expectations by Charles Dickens
On Christmas Eve, Pip is visiting his parents' grave when he meets an escaped convict and agrees to steal some food for him. So begins a relationship that will last as Pip grows into a man and is given opportunities to better himself. The character who made the greatest impression on me as a child – as I read the abridged version from the school classroom trolley – was Miss Havisham, a wealthy spinster who still wears her wedding dress years after she was jilted.

Jane Eyre by Charlotte Brontë
'Do you think, because I am poor, obscure, plain and little, I am soulless and heartless? You think wrong!' A

wedding that doesn't happen is also central to the plot of *Jane Eyre*. When we meet Jane, her parents are long dead of typhus and she is living with a cruel aunt and being tormented by her cousins. By the time she is standing at the altar, she has fallen in love with Mr Rochester, but her happy ending still lies far in the distance. I could endlessly reread this book, and it says something different to me every time.

Flambards by K. M. Peyton

Christina is both an orphan and an heiress, and has been passed around the family since the death of her mother. The book opens when she arrives to stay with her tyrannical uncle on his impoverished estate. He has two sons: Mark, who is hunting mad like his father, and Will, who is recovering after a riding accident, hates horses and longs to be an aviator. As Christina settles into her new life, she realizes that her uncle has plans to use her fortune to restore Flambards to its former glory.

Diana by R. F. Delderfield

When John Leigh goes to live with relatives in Devon after the death of his parents he meets Diana, the posh girl from the big house, and they embark on an unlikely friendship despite their different backgrounds. She renames him Jan after a character in *Lorna Doone* and he sets out to better himself so that he can be worthy of her. As the years pass, Jan realizes that he is not as central to Diana's life as she is to his. And then the war changes everything.

The Goldfinch by Donna Tartt

I first read this as an adult and felt a maternal interest in Theo, who is thirteen when an explosion in an art museum in New York tears his life apart. Out of the rubble he takes a tiny painting, *The Goldfinch* by the Dutch artist Carel Fabritius, and this one act of faith – or theft – will shadow him into adulthood. The novel flits between East and West Coast America and then to Europe, as a cast of eccentric characters struggle with existential dilemmas and try to make a living through art, drugs or gambling.

Dear Diary

These are my New Year's resolutions:

1. I will help the blind across the road.
2. I will hang my trousers up.
3. I will put the sleeves back on my records.
4. I will not start smoking.
5. I will stop squeezing my spots.
6. I will be kind to the dog.
7. I will help the poor and ignorant.
8. After hearing the disgusting noises from downstairs last night, I have vowed never to drink alcohol.

The Secret Diary of Adrian Mole aged 13¾
by Sue Townsend

I first met Adrian Mole on a shopping trip to York with my friend Isla, just before Christmas. Isla's mum Lin was an English teacher. She was very encouraging and liked my chatter, unlike some of my friends' parents who would comment that I had a lot to say for myself, in a way that made it clear they didn't think that was a good thing. Isla's family said 'supper' instead of 'tea', which impressed me, and I loved being in their house, which was full of books and had a smell I could never pin down but knew was sophisticated. Isla was a member of the Puffin Club and had an enviable scrapbook full of clippings of Princess Diana.

Isla's parents got divorced when we were seven and Mum said I should be extra kind to her. Then another friend's parents separated. 'You and Dad won't split up, will you?' I asked, and she told me not to worry.

I was rather fascinated and keen to observe adult behaviour. When my parents threw a party they invited Lin. She asked my dad if there would be any men for her to dance with.

'Big, rough Irishmen, Lin,' said Dad. 'They'll probably step on your toes.'

She laughed at that. Lin liked my dad and told me he was a rough diamond. She said once that she felt sorry for my mum for doing Open University, because it meant she had the work of college but none of the fun. When I repeated this to Mum, she said she'd been very happy doing her essays at the same time as bringing us up, but that I might like to go away to university like Lin had.

I was excited about our trip to York. We listened to the carol singers and ate cheesy jacket potatoes from a stall. We went into a huge bookshop, the biggest I'd ever seen, and Lin bought a copy of *The Secret Diary of Adrian Mole* to give to her other daughter for Christmas. Isla, being highly competitive and always on the lookout for opportunities to score off her sister, then used her pocket money to buy one for herself, so she would have the pleasure of noisily consuming it long before her sister would unwrap her own book on Christmas Day. I could see Lin was exasperated by this manoeuvre but couldn't work out what to do about it.

Later that day, we took turns reading the book aloud to each other in Isla's bedroom, she lying on the bed, me sitting on her beanbag. I was instantly entranced, but careful not to show it. Isla's competitive streak was not solely channelled towards her sister, and I knew if she saw how much I was enjoying it, there was a danger she'd snap the book shut. As it was, we read the whole thing that weekend, giggling over Adrian's obsession with measuring his thing.

I'm sure we missed many of the subtleties. One of the triumphs of Adrian Mole is that it can be appreciated on so many levels. It captures the teenage agony of having to go to school with a newly sprouted spot – the horror! – and skewers the desire of children for their parents to be conventional and caring. Adrian longs for his feminist mother to stay home, feed him spot-preventing vitamin C, and wear the Lurex apron he bought her for Christmas. It's an excellent example of a naive narrator: Adrian doesn't get why his mother and Mr Lucas are barricaded in the kitchen and won't open the door, but the adult reader completely understands what is going on.

Adrian himself is no stranger to the consolations of literature. As he writes during the divorce of his parents: 'I don't think anybody in the world can be as unhappy as me. If I didn't have my poetry I would be a raving loony by now.'

This is a book that is completely of its time – you can almost taste the boil-in-the-bag cod and hear the whirr of Nigel's Scalextric – yet also stands the test of time. I see a sadness now that I didn't notice when I was younger in the struggle of Adrian's parents to stay together, to find a way to navigate their differing needs and the impact of George Mole's redundancy. There's also something poignant in the innocence of the copies of *Big and Bouncy* that Adrian hides under his mattress in this age of internet porn, when lots of kids will first see sex on the phone screen of an older child in the playground. I'm now not only older than Adrian but also his parents. Hopefully I'll still be around to enjoy it when I reach the age of his grandmother. I wonder what I'll make of the entry where she goes around to the local bully, Barry Kent, and gets back the menaces money he's been extracting from Adrian.

Above all, it's funny in a glorious belly-laugh sort of way. Adrian's report of the disastrous school trip to the British Museum, where Ms Fossington-Gore loses control and Barry Kent absconds to Soho and is arrested for the theft of 'grow-it-big' cream and two 'ticklers', must be among the most guffaw-inducing pages in the whole of literature.

Adrian Mole sparked my lifelong interest in diaries both real and fictional. I've had numerous attempts at keeping them myself, though usually not for long. Many of my early diaries had an actual lock and key, and I used to make up stories, writing down imaginary conversations in which boys I'd never spoken to in real life asked me out, or kissed me, or walked me home from school. Every so often I would become so embarrassed by the inanities written by my younger self – sometimes only a few weeks ago – that I would shroud the diaries in layers of carrier bags and throw them in the outside dustbin, making sure to bury them deep in the rubbish so they wouldn't be disinterred.

I stopped making up diary entries as soon as I started having real entanglements with boys, but I remained a great chucker of my own words. What wouldn't I give for a peep in those old diaries now, I think, though perhaps it is no bad thing that they lie safely entombed in northern landfill.

There are many sequels to *The Secret Diary of Adrian Mole*. They are worth a look but they don't enthral me like the original, year after year. The edition I have now was released to celebrate the thirtieth anniversary of the first publication and includes an introduction from David Walliams, who rather neatly sums up the enduring appeal of Adrian Mole: 'Life is pain, and we all need to laugh.'

Fictional Diaries

There is something gloriously intimate about the novel in diary form. It makes it even easier to suspend disbelief, to forget that we are reading a made-up thing, and to immerse ourselves in the granular details of someone else's life. Of all the fictional characters who feel real to me, the diarists are among the most vivid.

The Diary of a Nobody by George and
    Weedon Grossmith

Charles Pooter is a clerk who lives with his wife Carrie in a house in Holloway called The Laurels. He worries about his son, Lupin, who engages himself to the vulgar Daisy Mutlar, joins a local amateur dramatics society and loses his job. Pooter has little self-awareness, and much of the humour comes from his high opinion of himself and his inability to read the world around him. The diary started off as a serial in *Punch* magazine in 1888, and still feels every bit as perceptive about the vanity and folly of human beings today.

Bridget Jones's Diary by Helen Fielding

Another funny fictional diary that opens with a list of New Year's resolutions (only one of which is eventually kept). Bridget is one of the greatest comic creations of all time, and this hilarious twist on *Pride and Prejudice* also affectionately illuminates the internal thought processes that can sit behind our desire to improve ourselves. I often reread it in those odd days between Christmas and New Year, and it never fails to cheer me up.

Any Human Heart by William Boyd

Logan Mountstuart experiences the events of the twentieth century to the full, keeping a record of his love affairs, his writerly struggles, and his meetings with Virginia Woolf, Evelyn Waugh, James Joyce and Picasso. During the war he knows both love and loss, and becomes entangled with the Duke and Duchess of Windsor. I could reread this book again and again. I love the way the fictional world blends with the real so that the reader can't tell where the edges are.

The Crimson Petal and the White by Michel Faber

We are beckoned down the darkest and dirtiest Victorian streets, following the fortunes of William Rackham. He is enamoured with Sugar, the daughter of a brothel keeper who has been used by men since her early teens. The diary is kept by William's wife, Agnes, who is so innocent that she understands neither menstruation nor pregnancy. It is always difficult to be brought face to face with the horrible things that human beings are capable of, but the triumph of the novel is that Sugar refuses to perpetuate the trauma she has suffered and the reader is left with some hope.

A Tale for the Time Being by Ruth Ozeki

An author called Ruth who lives on Desolation Sound finds a Hello Kitty lunchbox washed up on the shore. Inside the box is a diary and a collection of letters which draw us into the world of a Japanese schoolgirl, Nao, whose attempts to navigate her life make painful reading. This is a highly unusual and rewarding novel that covers a vast scope of disturbing subjects with great humanity, and continually loops back to the dilemma of how to live through difficult times.

Gone Girl by Gillian Flynn

When we start reading this novel, all we know about Amy Dunne is that she has disappeared. Her husband Nick is devastated, but alongside his blow-by-blow account of what happens after Amy vanishes – her forlorn parents, the suspicious police – we get to read Amy's diary, which paints a very different picture of their relationship. I don't want to give too much away, but this is one of those books that I wanted to read again as soon as I'd finished it to see how it was done.

The Grown-Up Section
of the Library

When I was a child, my family and friends were often aggravated that I would not want to come up for air once I had my nose stuck in a book. Isla came to stay for the weekend once, and was cross because I was immersed in *A Woman of Substance* by Barbara Taylor Bradford and would not put it down to entertain her. I just couldn't! Once I'd started on a story it was so hard to stop. It felt uncomfortable, as though the people were chattering in my head and I was abandoning them in a time of crisis.

I had fully graduated to the grown-up section of the library and was tearing my way through Agatha Christie. I adored the world she described – all those trains and cruises and country houses in which someone would suddenly die, and order would only be restored when Hercule Poirot or Miss Marple had sorted it out. I don't think it ever occurred to me that, if I'd been in one of those books, I'd have been a lumpen domestic sweeping the grates and serving the drinks rather than the daughter of the house. Still, Christie started me off on a lifelong relationship with classic crime that continues to console and delight.

To my great sadness we weren't taught history at school, but something called Humanities which involved making endless drawings of rock formations. I educated myself about kings and queens by reading Jean Plaidy, who had written so many books that she had a whole shelf to herself in the library. I was enraptured by Henry VIII and his desperate quest for a living son, and by Catherine de' Medici, poisoning her enemies and spying on her husband as he made love to his older mistress. Then I discovered Norah Lofts in the house of one of my teachers when I was babysitting. Lofts wrote about royalty, but also about everyday people. The trilogy that started out with *The Town House* told the story of the people who lived on a piece of land over several centuries. I read it again and again, marvelling at the way the narrative hopped between the characters and how a story often gained new depth by being told from another perspective.

I liked big chunky books full of story and emotion. Catherine Cookson was a favourite, and I read through *The Girl*, *The Mallen Streak* and *The Man Who Cried*. My dad cried a lot, whenever he heard about something sad. Both laughter and tears came easily to him, much more so than Mum. We always said in our family that Matty was like Mum – logical, calm, good at maths, and I was like Dad – emotional, chatty, fond of singing and stories. When we went to a funeral in Ireland I saw that the men cried in a way I couldn't imagine any of my English friends' fathers doing. There was lots of singing and storytelling, and Dad was proud that I would always have my turn.

I fell for R. F. Delderfield when *Diana* was televized on Sunday nights. I couldn't bear to wait for the next instalment so I got the book out from the library and read the whole thing, then moved on to *To Serve Them All My Days*, which is about Davy Powlett-Jones, a shell-shocked soldier from the Welsh valleys who is invalided home in 1917 and finds a measure of peace as a school-teacher, despite disapproving of the politics of most of his colleagues. As the Second World War approaches, both Davy and the reader feel a great weariness that yet more young men have to die.

Oh, the tears I have shed over these books! They are chock-full of the sort of social history I love – what education was offered, how local papers were run, the way women spoke about periods and pregnancy and careers – and are powerful page-turners with plenty of gasp-out-loud plot twists.

There was sex galore in *The Thorn Birds* by Colleen McCulloch, which tells the story of Meggie Cleary, the youngest of a large family, who lives on a sheep station in Australia with her rich and scheming Aunt Mary. She falls passionately in love with the priest, Father Ralph de Bricassart. Perhaps it was *The Thorn Birds* that wound my Aunt Kitty up so much. She came over from Ireland to stay with us one summer, and took my dad to task for letting me read dirty books. 'She'll ruin her eyes,' she said, 'and her morals!'

Aunt Kitty was always trying to get me to stop reading and spend more time doing chores around the house. She told Dad I didn't know what elbow grease was, and continually remarked on how much I reminded her of one of his sisters who had run away to England and gone to the bad. The visit was not a success. I could see Dad wanted to show her how far he had come from the grubby little boy who needed to be deloused when he came to stay, but she remained resolutely unimpressed by his English life and his English kids.

There had been plenty of sex in the historical fiction I read – often whole plotlines rested on whether or not someone could get pregnant – but now I had started to read about what people actually did . . . These new books were huge, with shiny covers and the titles written in curly letters. Jackie Collins, Judith Krantz, Danielle

Steel – I raced through them, taking in the new information and puzzling over what a douchebag might be.

Then I discovered the joy of Jilly Cooper when I picked *Imogen* off the shelf. Imogen is a librarian and a vicar's daughter from Yorkshire who goes on holiday with her tennis player boyfriend to the South of France. I was a bit embarrassed when I returned *Imogen* to my local library and the woman behind the counter – who looked terribly old to me but may well have been the age I am now – said, 'Oh, this has a librarian in it, doesn't it. Is it good?' My face flushed. I had no idea how to respond and immediately thought of the sex scenes. Surely she was too old to be interested in that?

I read my way through all Jilly Cooper's novels – and her collections of journalism about life in Putney. Her characters were often readers, writers or journalists, and I ached for the glamour. I still love them and always think of them when opening a new jar of coffee, as one of Jilly's men says he likes virgins in the same way he likes popping the top on a new jar of Nescafé.

Riders blew my mind. At primary school we'd been taken up to Carlton Towers to see the hunt set off. It was freezing cold, the horses were enormous, and the men in their coloured coats took drinks from silver trays. That memory helped me imagine the world I was reading about, full of posh people and horses and sex. Rupert

Campbell-Black is a show jumper who is rich and very badly behaved but full of talent and charm. Helen Macaulay is an American in London trying to heal her broken heart after an affair with her English professor ended in an abortion, a breakdown and flunking out of college. England is cold, her boarding house smells of cats, and English men are a disappointment to her as none of them look like Darcy, Rochester or Heathcliff, or even like they wash their hair often enough. Helen works at a publisher but 'the initial bliss of being paid to read all day soon palled because of the almost universal awfulness of the manuscripts'. One of Helen's colleagues is a vegetarian called Nigel with a thin neck like a goose. He bombards her with leftist literature and takes her out for a day with his anti-fox hunting friends. When Rupert sees Helen, he tells her she is too good-looking to be out with the antis, and after he catches Nigel letting down the tyres of his horsebox he beats him up, steals his address book, finds Helen's number and calls to ask her out. Like Helen, the reader is intrigued. As the pages turn, Helen and the reader are attracted, captivated, repulsed but ultimately unable to resist. I shouldn't have loved Rupert so much, but I did.

Back in school we were reading *Jane Eyre*, and learning about the talented Brontë sisters living up on the moor and dying off one by one. Their father, Patrick, was

Irish and their mother, Maria, was Cornish, which I took as an indication that perhaps I could be like them and become a writer one day. Shakespeare was a torment as hardly anyone understood it, and time hung heavy for us all – no doubt including our poor teacher – as we inched our way painfully through *The Merchant of Venice*.

I don't think I realized that some books were supposed to be better than others, and I had no concept of highbrow versus lowbrow. My dad thought of reading as a magic power and it didn't (and still wouldn't) occur to him to consider some books inferior to others. I must have realized that I wrote essays about Jane Austen and not about Jilly Cooper, but I don't remember any sense that the books I devoured were trashy, or guilty pleasures, or anything like that. Perhaps I thought that old books were classics and worthy of study – Shakespeare, Dickens, Austen, the Brontës – and new books were just for fun.

When we studied Jane Austen, my Uncle Richard gave me his own hardback copy of *Pride and Prejudice* which had notes in his neat handwriting – I wish I still had it – and showed me an essay he'd written about her when he was at teacher training college. He referred to her all the way through as 'Miss Austen' so I did too. My teacher gave me an A+ for my essay, but ran her red pen through the 'Miss' and said it wasn't necessary.

I may well have read *Pride and Prejudice* fifty times since then and it never disappoints. Is it a love story? I suppose so, but I'm in it for the vain and selfish characters: Mr and Mrs Bennet, he so superior and she so silly and vulgar, and the frightful Mr Collins. 'Can he be a sensible man?' Lizzy asks her father, on reading his overblown letter. This is a line I often use myself when discussing various male politicians, or anyone who is behaving as though they are a person of great consequence. I love awful, jealous Caroline Bingley and have a big soft spot for boisterous Lydia, the youngest and boldest sister, who runs off with Mr Wickham and lives in sin with him when she is only fifteen. We are not supposed to approve of her, but the older I get the more I think it is important to embrace our inner Lydia, rather than only trying to be as good as Jane or as likeable as Lizzy.

I didn't realize it at the time, but perhaps one of the reasons Jilly Cooper was such a delight to me was that her women were gleefully enjoying sex and even committing adultery and getting away with it. Literature in general, or everything I'd read up until then, rather seemed to punish women who had a sexual appetite. In my beloved Anne books, Ruby Gillis had too many beaux and ended up dead of consumption as the handsomest corpse Mrs Lynde had ever seen. It's difficult not to see that as a punishment for all that flirting. Succumbing to desire didn't work out well for Anna Karenina or Emma Bovary either.

You'll be relieved to hear, dear reader, that I don't intend to go into the details – but suffice to say, literature did nothing to prepare me for real life in this regard. I never encountered anyone remotely like either Gilbert Blythe or Rupert Campbell-Black or Mark Darcy, or even Mr Wickham. Everyone said D. H. Lawrence was sexy, but I thought the sex bits in *Lady Chatterley's Lover* were weird and kept having to reread whole sections of *The Rainbow* trying to work out whether or not they'd actually done it.

A couple of years after reading *Riders*, I had a boyfriend who was in the Socialist Workers Party and was always talking about marches he'd been on, though he never actually went on any in the months I knew him, and his activism seemed confined to slagging everyone off and shouting at the police when drunk. If only I had realized at the time how much he was like Nigel and I was like Helen, longing for a more interesting and glamorous life.

The Enduring Consolations of Crime

Perhaps all early readers are conditioned to enjoy crime fiction by reading Enid Blyton's stories. I have never fully understood why I enjoy mysteries so much – maybe it's something to do with order being restored by the end. Rereading an Agatha Christie feels like doing a cryptic crossword but with none of the effort. Here are the first outings of some of the detectives I most enjoy. There's nothing troubling, gruesome, or too modern here.

The Mysterious Affair at Styles by Agatha Christie
Written in 1916 and published in 1921, here is our first look at the legendary Hercule Poirot through the eyes of his friend, our narrator, Captain Hastings: 'Poirot was an extraordinary-looking little man. He was hardly more than five feet four inches, but carried himself with great dignity. His head was exactly the shape of an egg, and he always perched it a little on one side. His moustache was very stiff and military. The neatness of his attire was almost incredible; I believe a speck of dust would have caused him more pain than a bullet wound. Yet this quaint dandified little man who, I was sorry to see, now

limped badly, had been in his time one of the most celebrated members of the Belgian police.'

The Murder at the Vicarage by Agatha Christie
When the vicar of St Mary Mead reproaches elderly Miss Marple for gossiping, she says, 'You are so unworldly. I'm afraid that observing human nature for as long as I have done, one gets not to expect very much from it. I dare say the idle tittle-tattle is very wrong and unkind, but it is so often true, isn't it?' When Colonel Protheroe is shot dead in the vicar's study, it is Miss Marple who will uncover the criminals. Over the course of her long career she credits her wisdom to the fact that 'One does see so much evil in a village.'

The Secret Adversary by Agatha Christie
Tommy and Tuppence make their first appearance in this stirring adventure involving stolen documents and global conspiracies, set just after the Great War when they are both on their uppers. Unlike Poirot and Marple, Tommy and Tuppence age in real time which adds a pleasing dimension. They go on to be private detectives in *Partners in Crime*, are middle-aged spies in *N or M?*, and are still solving mysteries in their old age in *By the Pricking of My Thumbs* and *Postern of Fate*, the last novel

Christie wrote. It was published in 1973, the year of my birth.

Grey Mask by Patricia Wentworth
I'm a big fan of Miss Silver, who quotes Tennyson at her clients – 'Trust me in all or not at all' – and who often promotes a love affair at the same time as solving a crime. These are gentle mysteries full of fascinating details about rationing, blackouts and how telephone lines used to work. *Grey Mask* isn't the best but it's an enjoyable read, and if I were embarking on any series I think I'd start from the beginning.

Whose Body? by Dorothy Sayers
When a body is found in a bathtub, Lord Peter Wimsey gets involved and uncovers a tale of jealousy and revenge. The poshness of Lord Peter used to get on my nerves, but then I read an interview with Sayers in which she said she'd been very poor when she created him and enjoyed giving him the spending power to go to art auctions and drive around in fancy cars. *Whose Body?* is the first but I do prefer them from *Strong Poison* onwards, once Harriet Vane, a lady author accused of murdering her lover, comes into the picture. My favourite is *Gaudy Night*, published in 1935, and so interesting on whether women have to choose between family and intellectual life.

Cover her Face by P. D. James

Adam Dalgliesh is a poet as well as a policeman. I've read everything P. D. James wrote and love the way her characters are always quoting Shakespeare at each other over dead bodies. When I was first reading her novels, I thought that people like that must exist out in the actual world and wanted to find them. I have reluctantly come to the conclusion that Shakespeare-quoting policemen-poets are not terribly prevalent in real life.

A Morbid Taste for Bones by Ellis Peters

Brother Cadfael saw the world as a soldier in the Crusades and knew the love of women before becoming a monk at Shrewsbury Abbey. In this mystery, some of Cadfael's less fair-minded brothers are intent on claiming the bones of a Welsh saint as their own. This is a wonderful series that shows human beings at their best and worst. Cadfael's reassuring presence as he tends his herb garden, makes gentle jokes, and so often succeeds in tempering life's unfairness, is highly soothing.

Bonjour Tristesse

In 1989, when I was sixteen, we moved into the Bell and Crown in Snaith – just opposite the library – and Dad traded dirty work underground for pulling pints in his own pub. I felt like a character in a Norah Lofts novel, and would go down into the cellar – the oldest bit of the building, which dated from 1633 – and imagine what might have happened there in times gone by.

I took to bar work like I was made for it. I loved the chat and the jokes and meeting so many new people. Fridays and Saturdays were hectic and mainly about serving drinks as efficiently as possible, but on week nights we had teams who played games. I joined up and played darts on Monday and Wednesday nights, and often went along with the men's team on Thursdays. I learnt to play dominoes, too; a game called Fives and Threes that was essentially a grown-up version of Fizz Buzz, but now I could manage the sums. I most loved the conversations that happened around the matches.

Dad often said he felt like a priest in the confessional box as people would tell him their secrets, but most of what I learnt was gleaned by eavesdropping. I kept it to myself. I wasn't interested in exposing anyone's behaviour but felt privileged to be able to learn about people from life as well as from books. In Agatha Christie novels, the lower orders are often rendered so invisible by their function or uniform that you could commit a crime by dressing up as a butler, housemaid, policeman or steward and feel confident that no one would look you in the eye or see you as a person. Being a barmaid offers similar anonymity. People often forget that you have ears and a brain as well as hands to pour the drinks, so they chat freely in front of you in a way they never would if the role hadn't made you invisible. So my ears and my eyes were out on stalks; I already knew that one small village could teach you everything you needed to know about life, because that was how Miss Marple was so wise.

It was fascinating to witness the behaviour of adults from behind the bar as they had no idea what they gave away about themselves, especially after a few drinks. Sometimes I knew that an affair was going to happen before the protagonists did. By this time I'd learnt that older people were definitely still interested in sex, and almost as likely as my peers to be getting off with each other in an alleyway or a car. The only difference was that they'd be trying to keep it secret from their spouse rather than their parents.

Very few people in this new world read books: 'Book learning won't get you a husband,' said a customer to me one day, when I told him I wanted to go to university. 'You want to be careful you don't get left on the shelf.' They liked that I wanted to write, though: 'Put me in a book, love, plenty has happened to me. Though no one would believe it.'

Every day I took the bus to Scunthorpe where I did A levels in English, French and Theatre Studies. There, my world was expanded in a different way. I felt a bit dim at first, a country mouse compared to these kids from big schools. Lots of their parents were teachers, which was the height of sophistication to me at the time, and I imagined they discussed poetry over breakfast. In an early essay I wrote about someone making a 'mental picture' and the teacher ringed it in red: 'Do you mean an image?' Yes! I did. I learnt lots of new vocabulary, including that to write notes on a page was to annotate it. The first time I tried this out – rather proudly, in reference to 'Mr Bleaney' by Philip Larkin – I got it wrong and said 'acetate' instead. I can still remember the hot flush of shame as everyone laughed.

It was going well, though. I got an A for my essay on *The Bell Jar* by Sylvia Plath and I trained myself to like olives, after reading an Alan Bennett play in which a woman does exactly that.

I couldn't believe the size of the library – it was as big as our school hall – and dived into my reading lists. My view of the world was enlarged as I read *The Swimming-Pool Library* and *Oranges Are Not the Only Fruit* and *I Know Why the Caged Bird Sings* and *The Color Purple* and *If This is a Man*. It was a brave new world. And then there was poetry: Philip Larkin, Sylvia Plath, Ted Hughes and Tony Harrison. Liz Lochhead came to visit us – the first time I saw an author in the flesh – and talked about finding poems in everyday life. She read us one that was a conversation she'd overheard in a changing room. After that I started writing down things that people said in the pub and wondering how I might make a story out of it, though I still thought that not enough happened to me. I yearned for excitement and adventure – not just because I wanted to live, but because I wanted to have things to write about.

The first book I read by Julian Barnes was *Metroland*. It opens in 1963, with the sixteen-year-old narrator Christopher trying to rise above the tedium of school and suburbia. Later in the novel, Christopher goes to Paris where he does research, lives in a studio flat with a creaky floor, falls in love, makes some friends and meets his wife. Could I do that too, I wondered? Live in Paris and go to art galleries and make friends and make love with real-life French people?

I'd read a library copy of *Metroland* but then I bought my own. The bookcase in my room above the pub was undergoing a metamorphosis, as slim books with white spines took over from the fat books with shiny covers. I read *A History of the World in 10½ Chapters* and loved it even more, especially the half-chapter on love, and would announce with great authority to anyone who would listen to me that Barnes was 'good on love'. I am inclined to look back rather sneerily at the arrogance of my younger self but maybe I shouldn't, because she was right. Barnes *is* good on love. Take this, for instance: 'We must be precise about love. Ah, you want descriptions, perhaps? What are her legs like, her breasts, her lips, what colour is that hair? (Well, sorry.) No, being precise about love means attending to the heart, its pulses, its certainties, its truth, its power – and its imperfections.' Isn't that good?

It's no wonder I fell for books, when in my real life the men I served in the pub would often feel free to ask me if the hair on the rest of my body matched that on my head. Anne Shirley hit her eventual husband Gilbert Blythe over the head with a slate when he called her

Carrots. My only recourse was to practise my withering stares and hope for a time when I could access more enlightened conversation.

Reading *Flaubert's Parrot* sealed my fate when it came to what to do next. I decided that I would study French at university so that I could have a year abroad in my Parisian attic and read *Madame Bovary* in the language in which it was written, while I loafed around drinking coffee and wine and becoming sophisticated.

Bonjour Tristesse was the first novel I read in French that I enjoyed. I had to struggle through *Viou* by Henri Troyat first but I didn't want to read boring stories about children. I wanted passion and sex and regret and I found them in *Bonjour Tristesse*. I can remember catching sight of my reflection in the bus window as I turned the final few pages. That's me, I thought. I'm reading a novel in French.

I was seventeen, the same age as the narrator, Cécile, and only a year younger than its author Françoise Sagan was when the novel was published. *Bonjour Tristesse* was a *succès de scandale* in France when it came out in 1954 and crossed the Channel the year after. The title literally translates as 'Hello Sadness', which sounds odd in English. Something like 'So, this is sadness' would capture it better.

There is great force and vigour in Cécile. Her mother died when she was two, which we know because she tells us that her father, Raymond, has been a widower for fifteen years. He is kind, generous and amusing, with a succession of sensuous, worldly mistresses who keep him entertained. Cécile takes it in her stride, but when Raymond announces that he plans to marry a sensible, older woman, Cécile fears that her freedom will be curtailed. She sets out to wreck the relationship and is far more successful than she could have imagined. *Bonjour Tristesse* is only 30,000 words long yet captures the arrogance and certainty of youth, and that moment when innocence is destroyed and the world reveals itself to be crueller and more complex than we could ever have imagined.

I'd like to leave things here and keep my seventeen-year-old self – curious, opinionated, open, lively, not as clever as she thinks she is, mad keen on adventure, wanting to experience life – frozen in time, but I have to tell you what happened next. In the summer after my first year at Scunthorpe, a couple of months after I became the youngest ever winner of the Snaith and District Ladies' Darts Championship and two weeks before his exam results were announced as the best in his school, my brother Matty was knocked over by a car on a dark road near the pub. He never recovered from his injuries, and in many ways nor did I. *Bonjour Tristesse*, indeed.

Pub Books

Landlords don't get a good press in literature. They are often greedy, lecherous, violent or in league with the underworld. Crime novels are good on pubs. Ian Rankin's detective Rebus spends a lot of time propping up the bar. I like the Cormoran Strike novels by Robert Galbraith, especially as the detective's local – the Victory in St Mawes – is near where I now live in Cornwall, and I used to drink in the pubs Strike frequents near his office in London. Georgette Heyer novels feature plenty of inns and coaching houses, and the publicans are often good salt-of-the-earth types. Pubs get a starring role in soap operas which show them at the heart of the community, as indeed ours was, and when I tried to write a novel with a pub at its heart I realized I was effectively writing a northern *EastEnders*. The Blue Boar is the pub in St Mary Mead, but of course Miss Marple never goes into it.

A Wayside Tavern by Norah Lofts
Lofts imagines the inhabitants of an inn from Roman times to 1975, which was when she finished writing it.

The One Bull starts out as a wine shop with a tessellated floor, becomes a coaching house and then a pub, before being turned into a restaurant. Over the years the family faces different challenges, from violent invasion to the opening of rival establishments or a change in the route taken by the mail coach. There's also plenty about pubs in Loft's Suffolk trilogy. She writes beautifully about the motivation and desires of ordinary people through the ages.

Jamaica Inn by Daphne du Maurier
After the death of her mother, Mary Yellan leaves Helford to live with her Aunt Patience and her husband, Joss Merlyn, the landlord of Jamaica Inn. Even as she travels there, everyone she meets warns her to stay away. The inn is a strange place and its landlord a rough, cruel and drunken man. This strange, unsettling novel was inspired when Daphne du Maurier was out riding with a friend on Bodmin Moor in the 1930s and came across the real-life Jamaica Inn.

La Belle Sauvage by Philip Pullman
In the first novel of Pullman's Book of Dust trilogy we meet our heroine Lyra as a baby. Malcolm, the boy who helps her, is the son of a landlord. His parents' pub is by the river and called the Trout. I recognize Malcolm as a

fellow publican's child; you have to always be ready to pitch in and help, and you get to see and overhear things that most children don't, which is often fun and sometimes alarming.

Les Misérables by Victor Hugo
Perhaps it says a lot about the sort of teenager I was, that when I went on my first holiday with friends rather than parents – to Mallorca when I was sixteen – I took a copy of *Les Misérables* with me, and read it in between dancing and drinking and getting sunburnt on the beach. Monsieur Thénardier is the roguish landlord brought to life for wider audiences in the musical. He and his wife always manage to profit out of any situation and are a glorious double act of villainy. Dad and I used to sing their song 'Master of the House' in the pub as part of the Sunday night sing-along.

Cakes and Ale by W. Somerset Maugham
More of this novel takes place in literary London rather than in pubs, but I've included it for the portrait of Rosie Driffield whose husband, Ted, will become famous as a writer in later life. Our narrator is still a schoolboy when he meets the Driffields and is fascinated by the gossip about Rosie, who has worked as a barmaid at the Railway Arms and the Prince of Wales's Feathers and doesn't

seem to realize how shameful that is. Rosie says, 'I had a rare old time when I was a barmaid, but of course you can't go on forever. You have to think of your future.'

The Moon Under Water by George Orwell
This is an essay in search of the perfect pub. Orwell wants to confine darts to the public bar so there is less likelihood of being struck by an errant one, which makes me wonder what sort of pubs he frequented as no decent player would endanger anyone, though a dart can occasionally bounce out at an odd angle. Another of his requirements is the type of barmaids who know their customers' names and take an interest in their lives. I was always such a one.

The Aftermath

When something of this magnitude happens – I now think of the accident as a grenade that exploded into my lovely little family – it is difficult to carry on with everyday life.

Matty didn't die on the night he was knocked over, but nor did he ever regain consciousness. In the early days, I'd often wake up thinking I'd dreamt the whole thing and would be filled with relief before cold reality reasserted itself. There was a mirror on my bedroom wall and I'd pull myself up, sit on the edge of the bed and look into my wild, sad eyes as I confronted again the truth of what had happened. Often there would be a mark on my face, a ledge pressed into my skin, from the book that I'd fallen asleep on. This would – ever so slightly, like a tiny chink of sunlight through dark clouds – cheer me just enough to get up and on into the day.

In the years that followed, I reeled around not knowing what to do with myself, but found alcohol an effective emotional anaesthetic. I couldn't write anything; I bundled up my diaries and chucked them in the rubbish skip out at the back of the pub. Books helped, not least because I didn't like to get so drunk that the words swam. I couldn't bear to be alone with my thoughts so needed to be able to read until I went to sleep, light still on. A few hours later I'd wake up, still clutching the book.

There wasn't a specific book that helped me survive that time; it was more the act of reading itself that became a life raft, allowing me to stay afloat and keep my head above the water. Often people can be a bit snooty at the idea of books as a form of escapism, but I believe this is one of the great powers of literature: to comfort, to console, to allow a tiny oasis of – not exactly pleasure, but perhaps we could think of it as respite, when we feel we might otherwise drown in a sea of pain. I was reading for distraction rather than life lessons, and would churn my way through my charity shop collections of Agatha Christie and Georgette Heyer, who I'd picked up for romance – the covers were rather bodice-rippery – but appreciated for her wit and charm. Ellis Peters's Brother Cadfael mysteries were very soothing, too. I'd read through them and then start again at the beginning.

The writer I most remember discovering around this terrible time is Mary Wesley. *Not That Sort of Girl* opens in the aftermath of Ned Peel's death as his widow, Rose, looks back over her life, which she has spent in love with someone else. Most of the book is set during wartime, with boatloads of glorious detail – from the long, hot days in September 1939 when 'Whitehall wrapped itself in sandbags and the population of London began to dress in khaki and blue' through to Dunkirk, where Ned collects gooseberries in his tin hat, and the moment towards the end of the war when Rose and her lover Mylo are lying in bed in a borrowed flat in Chelsea and hear the new, sinister noise of a V1 rocket 'doodling its noisy way across London to explode in Harrow'.

It was a long way from Snaith and Scunthorpe, and I loved the details of how the posh people lived in the country and in London. Ned takes Rose to Cartier to choose her engagement ring and buys lingerie for her from the White House. He gets his hair oil from Trumpers or Penhaligon's. For books they go to Hatchards, though before her marriage Rose consults a sex manual for beginners in the lavatory at Foyles. Men eat potted shrimp and steak and kidney pudding with each other at their clubs. Ned takes his mistress to lunch at Quaglino's and she pockets some of his change while he is away from the table. When Mylo gets drunk at the Écu de

France – trying to dull the impression of smashed London and the disgust he feels at being asked to spy on the Free French operatives he is escorting across the Channel – he goes to Heppells, a chemist in Piccadilly, for an American pick-me-up. While in a prison camp in Spain he sends Rose a letter, most of which is censored. What is left reads: 'Stuck here playing bridge stop je n'oublierai jamais les lilas et les roses stop.'

Did it help me to read about people living in the shadow of war? I think it did. One of my problems in real life was that no one my age seemed to know much about suffering. I felt cut off from my contemporaries with their chat of exams and gap years and misbehaving boyfriends whilst I was sitting next to my brother in hospital struggling with the realization that he was never going to get better. But in Mary Wesley's novels I found Polly, whose brother Walter drowns in his submarine, and Victoria, who got the news on the same day that her brother and her fiancé had both been killed. They were about my age and it helped me to feel less alone, even if the fellow members of my support group were fictional.

The very way that fiction works – the process of conflict and resolution at the heart of every story – means that novels are full of people encountering challenging situations and, usually, surviving them. Books are a masterclass in how to carry on.

The intensity of novels set in wartime is a big part of their appeal for me. I felt intensely alive as I knelt next to Matty in the road and sat by his bed in intensive care. The proximity of death can sharpen the senses, and the best war novels – or the ones I most enjoy – are the ones where life has an added texture precisely because it is so fragile. As a reader, I enjoy the way that war often liberates characters from normal rules. Morals go out of the window as people try to cram in everything life has to offer while they still can. We may be dead tomorrow, goes the thinking, so why not go to bed together today?

Wesley's novels are full of people drinking stout and eating oysters; Ned and Rose have a dozen each when they lunch at Wiltons after Ned's leave. Rose is feeling ill, so she watches Ned drink two pints of Guinness and eat her brown bread and butter as well as his own, before she goes with him to the station and kisses him on the draughty platform as the guard blows his whistle. Ned goes off to war and Rose goes home to have pneumonia. Her recuperation will also involve oysters.

'We're like characters in a Mary Wesley book,' I said to my dad, as we shared a plate of oysters at Cronin's in Crosshaven on the south coast of Ireland. It was a couple of years after Matty's accident and we were visiting Dad's family. On the way back to the ferry, we spent a night in Dublin and went to see Brendan Behan's *Borstal Boy*. It was a joyous, exuberant performance and we laughed. We were the walking wounded, grievously damaged from the shrapnel of the explosion that had laid Matty low, but we were trying to stumble on, and to appreciate love and jokes wherever we could find them.

I did resist carrying on with normal life. I wanted to look after Matty for as long as he needed and then become a nurse – a ridiculous idea, I'd make a terrible nurse – but my parents were keen for me still to go to university, so I decided on Leeds as it was where Matty had been in hospital for nine months, and that made me feel close to him.

Leeds was only a half-hour drive from Snaith but the experience of going to university was Narnia for me, a doorway into another world where people, like my new best friend Sophie, might actually have been to boarding school and played lacrosse. Up until then, the most cultured people I knew were teachers and their kids. Having grown up being teased for having a posh voice and using long words, being told I was too clever for my own good, too full of myself, too keen on the sound of my own voice and so sharp I'd cut myself, it was a bit of a shock at Leeds to find I was nothing special and, compared to the new people I was meeting, I was not only commonplace but common. I learnt that 'Where did you go to school?' was not a question about geography and got used to being congratulated that I was well spoken for someone who'd been to a comprehensive. I watched other common people reinvent themselves – there was an Alan who started using his less plebeian middle name of Daniel, and a Julie who became a Julia – but I largely stayed the same. Books like *Brideshead Revisited* by Evelyn Waugh and *Jill* by Philip Larkin had trained me to believe that the worst thing to do is to pretend to be other than you are. And Anne Shirley kept her feet on the ground despite feelings of overwhelm when she went to Redmond College in *Anne of the Island*. I did upgrade from Regal King Size to Marlboro Lights and start saying lunch instead of dinner and dinner instead of tea.

When I went home at Christmas, the customers in our pub would say how posh my accent had become; when I went back to Leeds, my fellow students would remark that I'd got 'terribly Yorkshire' over the holidays. It wasn't intentional. My voice morphed to match my surroundings and still does, though I always kept my vowel sounds and – unlike Alan and Julie – I carried on rhyming glass, grass and bath with ass, not arse.

I learnt more new words and read more books and made a few friends, though I still found real-life relationships much harder to comprehend than those in books. Books were so forgiving and kept me company without making demands. Sometimes they changed my worldview – like *Ain't I a Woman* by bell hooks, which opened up new bits of my brain. I had to be a bit careful, though. I went completely mad trying to write an essay on *American Psycho* – I couldn't cope being up close to so much cruelty and violence.

I had my year in France, where I did not become sophisticated or fall in love with any French people or write in an attic, though I did live in a little studio flat in a small seaside town that had been a D-Day landing beach. There was a second-hand bookshop in Caen that was also a cafe – a radical concept at the time – and you could read from their shelves while drinking coffee so I'd go there all day, get through a couple of books, and then buy another to take home. I read *The Blue Bicycle* and its three sequels by Régine Deforges. These were addictive page-turners about the impact of the Second World War on a family of winemakers. They were rather like *Gone with the Wind*. The Scarlett O'Hara character was called Léa Delmas and was hungry for experiences, food and sex. She went on to get plenty of everything, despite the privations of wartime and being in love with her soppy neighbour rather than the highly exciting bad boy François Tavernier.

The book that I now associate most with my time in France is *Fear of Flying* by Erica Jong. I bought it from the English section of the second-hand bookshop and read about Isadora Wing eating peaches as she drove around Europe as part of her quest to work out how to live. I loved the gutsy way Jong wrote about bodies and periods and sex, though most of the sex in the book is not very good and Isadora's dreams of encountering the perfect zipless fuck don't come true. I also loved the way she wrote about fear, about being frightened of everything, and about how life, unlike books, has no plot.

My last year at Leeds went well. I lived with Sophie in a little house on Delph Lane, and she introduced me to her friend John with whom she had just spent a year in Moscow. He had stories galore about travelling around Russia with the MP he worked for, and how he'd become friendly with a man on the Trans-Siberian Express who told him, at the end of the six-day journey, that he was a mercenary and offered to kill someone for John for free.

John was amazed at the way I read and said he'd never known anyone who read so much or so quickly, or so widely. He was aghast at how badly I treated my books and how tatty they were from being dropped in the bath. He also suggested I spent rather too much time reading in the bath, and should get out a little and try a bit of life. So I did, and to my great surprise, in his company I began to find it almost enjoyable.

After graduating, I worked in the pub for a bit and then moved to London to be with John, who had got a job working for a recruitment company that specialized in Russia and emerging markets, and spent his days trying to persuade people to go and work for soft drinks or tobacco companies in Kazakhstan or Uzbekistan. We lived in a top floor flat on Little Russell Street opposite the British Museum. They were doing big construction work there, and I'd lie in bed hungover and listen to the noise of the builders. Sophie had trained to be a journalist, and sometimes I'd go on jobs with her and sit next to her in a courtroom watching her write in shorthand. I loved tagging along to the pub and meeting other journalists and photographers – blunts and snappers, as they referred to each other. They were often very funny and it felt novelistic to me. Sometimes I thought that I too would like to be a journalist, but it seemed a big thing to aspire to.

Apart from John and Sophie, my saving grace was Camden's libraries. There was a branch near King's Cross and another on Theobalds Road. I'd spend hours in there and then take a huge pile of books home. Sometimes I sent myself a bit crazy with reading. I worked out that the maximum number of new books I could cope with in a day was three. If I pushed it beyond that, I'd become confused about what was real and what was invented and start imagining myself into plotlines. I'd dream that what had happened to the people in the books had happened to me, and would wake up terrified and distressed.

I binged my way through the whole of Pat Barker's Regeneration trilogy in a weekend. As ever, I was taking a peculiar comfort in reading about people living in extreme circumstances. I had associated Matty with the shell-shocked soldiers of the Great War since reading 'Futility' by Wilfred Owen. Owen is a character in *Regeneration* along with Siegfried Sassoon, who makes some corrections to Owens's poem 'Anthem for Doomed Youth.' I couldn't stop reading, but by the end I was almost hallucinating and then had strange dreams for days.

I liked audiobooks and used them as bait to get me out of bed, to do chores in the flat or errands that involved the outside world. One day I took out an abridged audiobook of *Possession* by A. S. Byatt. After a few minutes of listening, I knew I couldn't bear to miss a word and dashed off to the Waterstones on Gower Street to buy the book. *Possession* is full of my favourite literary ingredients: letters and diaries forming part of the story, fictional writers and poets, different time frames. Roland is a lowly researcher into a famous poet called Randolph Henry Ash, and discovers some drafts of a letter Ash wrote to a lady poet. Who was she, and did Ash ever finish the letter and send it? Roland's quest to uncover her identity leads him to Maud Bailey, and together they embark upon a highly satisfying literary mystery. I read it on the train up to Yorkshire to visit my parents, turning the pages as we sped through Peterborough then Grantham and pulled into Doncaster.

Eight terrible years elapsed between Matty's accident and his death. I still feel a bit surprised that I survived them, and so grateful to books because I have no idea how I would have coped were I not able to escape into other worlds.

O Brother, Where Art Thou?

Unable to bear the thought of a real-life support group, I found my own on the shelves. I often saw myself in these stories of sibling loss, many of which are autobiographical. It always helped to know that others had walked through the fire and – though not undamaged – come out the other side.

The Travelling Hornplayer by Barbara Trapido
'Early on the morning of my interview, I woke up and saw my dead sister.' Ellen and Lydia's father calls them Gigglers One and Two, and is inclined to treat them like two halves of the same pantomime horse. When Lydia runs out in front of a car without looking left or right, she is killed and Ellen is bereft. In the past, people confused them for each other because they looked alike, but now nobody does because 'The Lydia that once lived is dead in both of us.' I read this book the year Matty died and could see both of us reflected in the knockabout behaviour of the girls before the accident, and myself in Ellen's stunned reality when she is left alone.

All My Puny Sorrows by Miriam Toews

'Public enemy number one for these men was a girl with a book.' Sisters Yoli and Elf grow up in a Mennonite community 'rigged for compliance'. Now in their forties, Elf, a renowned concert pianist, is in hospital after her latest attempt to take her own life. Can Yoli make her want to live? Or be persuaded into helping her to die? The astonishing thing about this precise and beautiful book is how funny it is, and how the pain and joy of life are faultlessly woven together.

Family Life by Akhil Sharma

'I had not fully understood that going to America meant leaving India.' Life changes for Ajay and his family when they leave Delhi for New York, but just as they are getting used to carpets, elevators and glass doors that slide open when you stand in front of them, Ajay's brother Birju has an accident that leaves him irrevocably damaged. As Ajay's parents struggle to cope with the transformation of their clever son, Ajay is left adrift and unsure of how to live in this strange new world.

26a by Diana Evans

Twins Georgia and Bessi Hunter grow up in Neasden in the attic of the family house, with their homesick Nigerian mother, their drunk and sweary English father, two other sisters, and a hamster called Ham. They watch the wedding of Charles and Di and revel in their 'twoness in oneness', but growing up brings difficulties for the twins who feel each other's pain. By the time the nation is mourning the people's princess, the Hunter family is engulfed by its own tragedy.

The Impossible Lives of Greta Wells by Andrew
    Sean Greer
'It is almost impossible to capture true sadness; it is a deep-sea creature that can never be brought into view.' New York, 1985: Greta can't get over the loss of her adored twin brother Felix to AIDS just after their thirty-first birthday. When she finds herself catapulted into other eras by electroconvulsive therapy, Greta meets other versions of herself and Felix, and we see that she will do anything to live in a world where she can see her twin in the flesh and not just in her dreams.

A Girl is a Half-Formed Thing by Eimear McBride
'For you. You'll soon. You'll give her name. In the stitches of her skin she'll wear your say.' We never know the name of our narrator, but the 'you' she addresses is her brother, whose brain was damaged after the removal of a tumour. As I read this, I became more and more certain that the reason for the experimental language was that the

narrator was going to have to find a way of telling us that her brother dies, and that our existing language just isn't good enough, or is too well mannered, to be up to the job.

The Power of Magic

I'd expected to feel better after Matty's death, relieved that he was finally free, but I didn't. I stumbled and blundered and floundered as I cast around for ways to try to live. I considered getting out of life altogether, but it seemed a shitty thing to do to my parents. I married John because everyone else wanted that to happen – he'd proposed to me after an incident in a casino in Almaty where he thought he was going to be shot – but my mind was elsewhere and I sobbed for my lost brother even as I walked up the aisle.

I was trying to write and didn't have a proper job, though I did a few shifts behind the bar at the Plough on Museum Street. Deep down, I knew it wasn't good for me not to be working, and I'd have sporadic attempts to get myself employed that always went wrong. Once I answered an ad for a marketing job in the paper, but when I got there it turned out to involve going door to door trying to get people to change their electricity supplier. I enjoyed hanging out with John and his colleagues in the pub and considered becoming a recruitment consultant myself, but had a horrible interview with a woman who clearly thought I was useless, which made me increasingly anxious. She fed back that I had not made a good impression – she said I hadn't made eye contact with her – and I couldn't bear to try again. Temping was a horror as I could hardly type or use computers, and my poor sense of direction meant I would get lost on my way to jobs and then be unable to navigate around huge office buildings. I knew that there was confidence and charm hidden somewhere inside me – I was a good barmaid – but could feel myself wilt under the beady eyes of carefully made-up office manager types who seemed able to assess my flat shoes, bitten nails and lack of skills in one devastating glance.

Meanwhile, John's career was going well and he spent most of 1999 sending IT people who were Y2K specialists all over the world. We spent Millennium Eve in the Bell and Crown and woke up to find that nothing had changed.

Back in London, we celebrated my twenty-seventh birthday by going to see *Sing-a-Long-a Sound of Music* with Sophie and our friend Rob. Everyone in the audience belted out the songs and booed every time the Baroness appeared. Rob gave me a brown paper package tied up with string and I opened it to find the first two Harry Potter books.

The next morning, hungover, I opened *Harry Potter and the Philosopher's Stone*. Everyone knows the story of the unloved orphan boy who lives in a cupboard under the stairs, and finds out on his eleventh birthday that he is not only a wizard but famous in the wizarding world. I raced through it, entranced by the details of this parallel magical universe where Harry goes off to Hogwarts to learn from headmaster Albus Dumbledore. He meets Ron and Hermione on the train, is put into Gryffindor House by the Sorting Hat, and has to deal with the enmity of Professor Snape and Draco Malfoy.

When I got to the Mirror of Erised I cried fat tears all over the book. As Dumbledore explains to Harry, when you look in the Mirror of Erised you see no more or less than your heart's deepest desire. Ron, always overshadowed by his older brothers and his famous friend, sees himself as head boy and captain of the Quidditch team. Orphan Harry sees himself with his parents. People can go mad, Dumbledore warns, longing for what cannot be.

When I finished, I immediately picked up *Harry Potter and the Chamber of Secrets* and then headed off to Waterstones to buy *The Prisoner of Azkaban*.

This writer really understands death and depression, I thought, as I read about the Dementors, strange creatures who suck the joy out of humans and make them feel they can never be happy again. I read on and watched Harry try to cast a Patronus – to concentrate so hard on a single happy memory that he could charge down the Dementor with white light. When Harry passes out in front of his classmates, Professor Lupin reassures him that he is not crazy, but that when the Dementors come, his mind flies to his worst memory, the death of his parents. I began to sense a glimmer of how my own depression seemed to function, in that when my mood plunged I would endlessly play my most distressing memories of Matty in my head and berate myself for my shortcomings. I didn't know how to cast a Patronus to keep the gloom away, though both reading and alcohol continued to be effective distractions.

A couple of months later, John was asked to take a job in New York and we decided to go for it. We arrived on 4 July 2000 and settled into a flat – we learnt to say apartment – in Chelsea. I loved New Yorkers and how easy it was to strike up conversations with strangers. I was so happy when a woman stopped me in the street to tell me she liked my shoes. I'd never thought of myself as looking Irish before – though I knew I looked like many of my cousins – but Irish Americans would clock me as one of their own in bars and I made several new friends that way. There was a whole new bar etiquette to learn and I enjoyed training up visiting friends on how to order a martini – be specific – and the importance of tipping.

At the end of our street there was an enormous Barnes & Noble, and I queued up to buy *Harry Potter and the Goblet of Fire* when it came out and stayed up all night reading it.

I became almost nocturnal, sleeping during the day and trying to write a novel of my own at night, but I kept getting stuck. I thought the fact that I found writing hard meant I wasn't talented. Surely if it was important enough to me to do it, or if I was good enough, I'd find it easier to get the words down rather than being so easily led astray into other people's books. By the time we left New York a year later, the bookshelves were full of paperbacks – mainly historical fiction or cosy crime that I had bought by the basket-load at Barnes & Noble. I had got into Bernard Cornwell and read the Sharpe books, and then an excellent Arthurian trilogy which began with *The Winter King*. I left them all behind. The only book I still have from that time is a great tome called *The Book of Great Books: A Guide to 100 World Classics*. I don't remember doing it, but little pencil ticks check off those I've read.

John was ready to have children, but I couldn't see that I would ever be fit to be a mother. The Dementors were too close to me and I didn't feel confident I'd be able to keep fighting them off. I was stuck staring in my own Mirror of Erised, in which I saw me and my brother laughing and joking together. I couldn't commit to life, or do anything other than grieve or try to blot out the pain with drink. After a couple of years, the marriage ended sadly but amicably. John and I have never stopped loving each other, just in a different way.

I knew I needed to get a job when I got back to London, and dreaded a return to the humiliating temping roles where I'd fuck up the switchboard or not be able to work out the fax machine. The only thing I knew how to do was read books. I thought about publishing or journalism but everyone said they were impossible to get into. I didn't fancy being a barmaid or a waitress but I did know how to serve people and was good with customers. So I decided to try to get a job in a bookshop.

I made online applications to everywhere I could think of but didn't receive a single response. Then one night I was round at Sophie's mum's house and she said Harrods had a book department. Why didn't I go in and ask? It seemed mad for me to go somewhere as posh as Harrods, but it was the only place I could think of that I hadn't tried. So Sophie lent me a suit and I found my way to the second floor of Harrods – and there a whole new world opened up.

Series Books

When I began my Harry Potter journey, only three books had been published so I had to wait until the next instalment to carry on reading. Perhaps because of starting out with Narnia and then plunging into school stories, I do love a tale that just goes on and on. Here are the first books in some of my favourite series. What could possibly be better than a book? A whole boxed set of them!

A Discovery of Witches by Deborah Harkness
Imagine Harry Potter for grown-ups with extra helpings of history and science. I love this trilogy about a witch and a vampire in search of a lost manuscript. Diana is such a powerful witch that her parents spellbind her for her own safety just before they are killed. The way magic sparks out of her makes me think of the way repressed emotions burst out unbidden, and I now think the whole thing is a metaphor for the way we hide parts of ourselves to better conform to society.

March Violets by Philip Kerr

Berlin in 1936, and wisecracking cop turned private investigator Bernie Günther is in constant danger as he searches for the many people who have gone missing in the early days of the Reich. Originally a trilogy that spanned the years 1936–47 and narrated the rise and fall of Hitler, there are now fourteen books to enjoy. The action stretches into the future, but often involves flashbacks to the war and Bernie's struggles to stay alive in a regime that he hates. The language sizzles and the books are full of unmissable one-liners like: 'I'm no longer young enough, nor quite thin enough, to share a single bed with anything other than a hangover and a cigarette.'

My Dear I Wanted to Tell You by Louisa Young

The title of this novel is taken from the form letter sent home by wounded troops during the Great War. Riley Purefoy is horribly disfigured in the trenches and his captain, Peter Locke, is damaged in less obvious ways. The series explores the after-effects of war on the combatants and their families, and the third novel, *Devotion*, takes us to Italy in the 1930s where it is all too easy for Nenna and her Jewish family to ignore the threat posed by Mussolini.

Never Mind by Edward St Aubyn

We first meet Patrick Melrose when he is a boy living with his rich American mother and cruel aristocratic father in the South of France. There are two more novels in the original trilogy, and then St Aubyn went on to write *Mother's Milk* and *At Last*, to bring the story to a triumphant close. Terrible things happen in these novels but the writing is so precise and elegant that somehow the reading experience soothes as well as disturbs. And they are – especially *At Last* – extremely funny.

My Brilliant Friend by Elena Ferrante

The novel opens in the present when our narrator Elena finds out that her friend Lila has gone missing. Elena knows that Lila has been wanting to vanish for years: 'And since I know her well, or at least think I know her, I take it for granted that she has found a way to disappear, to leave not so much as a hair anywhere in this world.' Elena decides to write about their intimate and tangled friendship, forged against the backdrop of the corrupt and often violent neighbourhood of Naples.

The Girl Who Reads

I was in the Blackbird on Earl's Court Road with Sophie when the manager of the Waterstones in Harrods rang to offer me a job with an immediate start.

'You'll be our first Christmas temp,' he said.

'I hope I sounded enthusiastic rather than pissed,' I said to Sophie after I hung up. We were already a few pints in.

'How much will you get paid?' Sophie asked.

I told her.

'That's not very much,' she said.

'No,' I said, 'but I can pay rent and eat. And I only really need money for books and we can borrow them from the shop, as long as we only take one at a time.'

My heart pounded when I presented myself at Harrods for induction training. There were strict rules about dress code and shop floor behaviours that made me think of those swimming pool notices about not running or jumping or making noise. We had to come in and out through a staff entrance across the street from the main building and decant our belongings into a locker. The only things we were allowed to take through the tunnel that led into the shop had to be carried in a see-through plastic bag. Women were allowed a small cosmetics purse, presumably so that we could be discreet about our periods. We could be searched at any time.

We were given a staff ID card in a little plastic case. The colour showed our place in the strict hierarchy at Harrods; mine was white, the least important. We were also taught about the carnation system, and encouraged to aspire to getting a flower to pin on our lapel; red was the highest. Carnation wearers could do various levels of responsible tasks like processing refunds, ordering change and closing down tills.

My first day on the shop floor passed in a blur. I was nowhere near as well read as I'd thought, nor had I grasped the scale of a bookshop and how many different subjects you had to know about. I got in a mess with Ordnance Survey maps, and made a fool of myself not knowing that guides for Madeira would be shelved with Portugal. A woman got cross with me because I didn't know which of the hundred cookbooks on the shelves would have a recipe for olive polenta.

And how my feet ached! I was complaining about it in a pub that night when someone at the next table said she could help. She got me to take my shoes off and showed me how to massage my feet – pressing really hard into the ball. It was like magic. I did it at breaktimes through my bookselling years and still feel grateful to that helpful stranger.

The second day was better, and by the third I was starting to feel like I knew what I was doing and that I had found the right place to be. I worked on the front desk, which suited me as I liked to have plenty to do and a good supply of people to chat to. 'It will be a baptism of fire,' said Angela, who had worked there for many years, and she and fellow bookseller Richard set about teaching me everything they knew with great humour.

There was a carnival atmosphere at Harrods. It was a tourist destination as well as a department store, so you'd be directing someone to the Diana Memorial one moment, then recommending the best in new fiction the next. We seemed to spend huge amounts of time talking to customers about the toilets. Some months earlier, Harrods had introduced a charge of £1 to go to the loo and received vast amounts of negative press. They repealed the policy but we still got plenty of enquiries along the lines of, 'Where are the toilets? And do I really have to pay a pound to use them?'

We were round the corner from the pet shop and often customers would turn up expecting to take home an exotic animal, as they would have been able to in the 1950s. We knew that the law had changed but it wasn't our job to get into that, so when people pitched up at the desk asking for a lion, I would direct them to the pet shop and wish I could eavesdrop on the ensuing conversation.

On the other side of the bookshop was Christmas World, a year-round festive shop, so working in the travel section involved listening to carols from dawn until dusk. People would come from far and wide at any time of the year to take home a Harrods bauble. I once overheard one of the girls who worked there complaining because the elves from Santa's Grotto were paid more than the other staff.

In the world of the bookshop, there was a whole new vocabulary to learn. 'Proofs' were advanced copies of soon-to-be-published novels that publishers would send out to booksellers and journalists to get them interested. Books would first be published in hardback. Each one would have a dust jacket and the inside covers were called 'endpapers'. I had always loved books that came with a ribbon sewed into the spine and learnt it was called a 'ribbon marker'. The paperback edition would come out around a year later and be smaller and cheaper. 'Unpacking' was the process of receiving boxes of books from publishers; 'shelving' or 'trolley work' was putting them out on display. The books needed to go into the A–Z section and also in piles on tables, depending on how many copies we'd ordered. The bookshelves were divided into bays and the free-standing units were called 'dumpbins', a peculiarly unpleasing name. I quickly learnt they were a perfect way of grouping together books that were connected.

When you faced a book out in a display, you'd write a little recommendation card to stick underneath it, encouraging people to buy it. One of my jobs was to refresh the 'staff recommends' bay. Some of my colleagues were a bit reluctant, so I said I'd write the card out for them so long as they'd choose a book. Initially I deliberated a long time over what to write, but then I got the hang of it. The cards didn't need to be lengthy and exquisitely crafted. A few heartfelt words went a long way. I loved writing the cards and was always delighted when a customer said they were buying something as a result.

One morning on the way to work, I was so engrossed in the new Minette Walters novel that I tried to carry on reading it as I walked along the street. I tripped over and cut my knee yet still only wanted to keep reading. I wrote that little story onto a recommends card and the copies flew off the shelves. I'd read on my breaks, and then take a book home every night and usually finish it before I went to bed. If a book was very short – like *Embers* by

Sándor Márai – I could finish it over lunch and break-time. I enjoyed there being purpose to my reading. It added another dimension: that as I was enjoying something I'd start thinking about which of my customers would like it.

Often I'd read late into the night because a book was just so good. *The Crimson Petal and the White* by Michel Faber, *Any Human Heart* by William Boyd and *Finger-smith* by Sarah Waters all deprived me of sleep and were so much fun to sell. 'It sure sounds pretty,' said a nice American lady, weighing *The Crimson Petal* in her hands, 'but it's too heavy for my suitcase.'

'Throw away some clothes,' I said, and she bought it.

'I really do think people should buy books rather than food,' I said to another customer. Though perhaps not rather than food for your children, we agreed.

It wasn't all larks. The main preoccupation of the Harrods management was theft, and they stalked the shop floor on the lookout for infractions and wrong-doing. The main feature of the staff entrance was a name-and-shame board that had photos of staff members who'd been caught stealing and details of their punishment. This made for a grim welcome to work. One day there was a notice in its place: 'The name-and-shame board has been relocated to the staff restaurant.' I wasn't sure that was much of a solution.

I was only the new girl for a couple of weeks as other Christmas temps started to arrive. I was chuffed to be given responsibility for training them. 'Tell them what you wish you'd known when you started,' said the manager.

Lizzie came from Hebden Bridge and we took to each other immediately. She was very keen to do staff recommends cards. She wrote one that said, 'I was enjoying this book so much it made me late for work,' but one of the Harrods big cheeses made us take it down.

Above all, I loved talking to strangers about books. Soon, I had regular customers who'd come in to see me and ask what was new. One posh elderly lady would lean her walking stick against the front desk and say, 'Where's the girl who reads?' I liked this, with its echo of Harry Potter; the boy who lived. Some booksellers didn't much enjoy interacting with customers, and would try to escape them by unpacking or working in the mail order room. I was rather the opposite, often falling into intense conversations with people I'd only just met. It reminded me of being in the pub, and the excitement of not knowing who would walk through the door and what story they might have to tell. I found it easy and enjoyable to be on friendly terms with customers. I'd just start chatting to them about whatever book they'd picked up or display they were looking at. One day my boss hauled me into his office to reprimand me: 'You shouldn't let your friends come in and distract you on the shop floor.' I'd been talking to someone I'd never met before but we'd obviously been having too good a time.

That first Christmas was brutal. Customers would take out their stress and unhappiness on us, and I cried three times on Christmas Eve. But it was still easier than working in pubs. 'At least we get to go home at 6 p.m.,' I said to my colleagues. 'Most of our customers are neither drunk nor violent. And there is zero chance I'll end up standing in the main street come midnight with no front windows left and covered in someone else's blood.'

The January sales challenged this optimistic outlook. There were stampedes through Harrods on Boxing Day as desperate shoppers tried to bag one of the limited numbers of cut-price TVs. We had to wear gaudy sashes and rosettes that said 'Sale' in big letters, and the customers were bargain-focused and less polite than usual, which made the days long and thankless. By my thirtieth birthday on 8 January I felt truly miserable. I walked down Finborough Road looking at the discarded Christmas trees that had been put out for the council to collect. Some of them still had stray bits of tinsel in the branches. The rain was coming through the holes in my shop girl shoes and I couldn't afford to buy a new pair until payday on the twentieth. I felt like I was stuck in the first chapter of a chick lit novel; the bit where everything has gone wrong and the heroine is at her lowest ebb. When were things ever going to get better? When was I going to get into chapter two and start working my way towards an uplifting ending?

Because I'd been hired as a Christmas temp, I had no idea if I'd be kept on and was frightened that this tiny niche I'd found for myself might be taken away. Luckily I was made permanent; the sale ended and there was the thrill of new books arriving.

I began to anticipate the moment I'd walk into the goods-in room and see something new on the trolley. After a while, I could feel a tingle in my fingers when I touched something that was going to be really good. The first time it happened was with *The Curious Incident of the Dog in the Night-Time* by Mark Haddon. I hadn't heard of the book before but when I picked it up – it had a jacket that looked like brown paper – I felt a distinct sensation in my fingertips. The same thing happened with *Notes on a Scandal* by Zoë Heller and *What I Loved* by Siri Hustvedt. I felt a bit strange and secretive about it, but I did tell Richard one day, when we were gossiping at the front desk in a lull between customers. We never looked at each other in these stolen moments, but stood side by side surveying the floor for customers and trading secrets in low voices. 'I get a tingle in my fingers,' I said to him. 'Do you think I'm mad?'

'No more than anyone else,' he said. 'I think you're a bit of a book whisperer.'

A favourite job was being in charge of the 'recently reviewed' table. I had to go through the weekend papers to see which books had created a splash and make sure they were easily available. Very few customers would come in and ask for exactly what they wanted by title and author. More often they'd say, 'I want that book about the boy and the tiger,' or 'You know, the one where the teacher has an affair with her student.' I enjoyed this as it was rather like being a contestant on a quiz show and I was usually up to speed, though one Monday morning around 11 a.m. a woman came in and was annoyed I didn't immediately know what book she was talking about.

'I can't believe you haven't heard of it,' she said. 'It was on *Start the Week* this morning.'

'But I wasn't listening to *Start the Week* this morning,' I said, 'I was here.'

One problem was that customers always thought – and who can blame them – that if a book had been reviewed in the paper or discussed on Radio 4 it would definitely be available to buy. They'd come in with the books section of their newspaper marked with asterisks and couldn't understand why some of them weren't yet out. I must have explained hundreds, even thousands, of times that books are often reviewed before their publication date.

'Well, that's a stupid system,' people would say.

'I know,' I'd smile, trying to indicate my complete lack of power in the situation, 'why don't you write to the *Sunday Times* about it?'

On Tuesday mornings before the shop opened, we'd have our staff meeting around my table and I'd run through the recently reviewed books, briefing everyone on what had been said about them. I was in the middle of this one morning when the PA system crackled and suddenly the voice of Harrods owner Mohamed Al-Fayed himself was boomed out to the whole shop, as he took issue with various things that had been said about him in the press. We had to stand still and listen, as there were rumours that the security cameras were used to make sure the staff attended to these broadcasts respectfully. It was hard not to get the giggles.

The job was surprisingly moving sometimes. I was asked to recommend something for a customer's friend undergoing chemotherapy – P. G. Wodehouse on audio – and we had a bit of a cry together. This was before Google, so people who wanted to find the right poem to read at a funeral would simply come in and ask. Often they'd tell me about the person who'd died and I'd note the fragile, jangly nature of the newly bereaved and feel glad that I could help them, even if only in a tiny way.

Often people would talk to me about their lives – I will never forget the woman who told me about leaving Berlin in 1938 as I was tracking down a copy of *Defying Hitler* by Sebastian Haffner for her. She was British and had gone over to work as a governess, then met and married a German. Their relief at getting back to England was checked when he was then interned and spent most of the war on the Isle of Man.

Spending time with customers often cheered me up. I preferred to be at work inhabiting my enthusiastic bookworm persona, rather than having to be in my own life trying to be myself – whatever that meant. On my days off I lay in bed reading and smoking. When I took holiday, I missed the solace of being surrounded by books. I was miserable and lonely, and after a few days I'd have to resist the urge to start up conversations with strangers on tubes and buses over what they were reading.

At work I felt useful and helpful and like there was a point to me. I had taken to wearing a green Harrods apron rather than my suit jacket, and I liked the way I felt purposeful as I carried stock around and tidied up, always on the lookout for customers I could help. Once a woman told me I'd restored her faith in human nature.

I can't remember what I'd done for her, but her kind words powered me through a rough time.

Sometimes very wealthy people would come in to order a library and leave it up to me to choose the books. That felt like power of a kind. Usually they'd want mainly photographic books, but I'd gently persuade them that a few shelves of fiction would add a nice touch, and was able to rehome some of my favourites in the hope that one day the library would get a visitor who would enjoy them.

Not all the customers were lovely, of course. Many of the people who shopped at Harrods were staggeringly rich and some of them wanted you to know it. As a barmaid, I'd never been keen on those men who waggled a £20 note in their fingers as though being able to see money might make you serve them more quickly. I felt the same about the people who would take their platinum or black Amex cards out of their wallets and rap them on the desk when they wanted attention.

A man with extreme nasal hair once got so cross with me when I wouldn't give him a refund for some old and tatty-looking Jeffrey Archer novels that he started tearing them up and throwing them at me. A woman kicked off because we hadn't heard of the new book by Gerald Durrell that was all over the papers. She'd worked her way through a couple of my colleagues, shouting at them that they were stupid. It turned out she meant Paul Burrell's book about Princess Diana. 'Yes, that's it,' she said, when I suggested it. 'I can't believe it took you so long.'

Sometimes there were misunderstandings. One day a Russian woman asked me to recommend the best in contemporary fiction. She was beautiful with perfect blonde hair. Something very modern, she said. I sent her off with a copy of *Notes on a Scandal* by Zoë Heller. It had just been shortlisted for the Booker Prize and I was rooting for it to win. I loved the way the story darkened as the narrator Barbara became increasingly sinister in her retelling of her colleague's affair with a schoolboy.

The perfect blonde came back the next day angry and in tears. 'How could you give me such a terrible book?' she said. 'It is pornography. I have a son.' She was shouting at me and other customers were staring. I apologized and offered to give her something else instead, but she just wanted her money back.

Later, smoking a fag on my break and still feeling shaky and bruised at being accused of peddling porn, I figured we had both understood different things from the word 'contemporary'. It taught me a lot about how what people say they want isn't always what they want, a lesson that continued to resonate both on and off the shop floor.

I wasn't always so wise. I once spent a long time with a man who wanted me to go through all our editions of the *Karma Sutra* with him, comparing the illustrations. I threw myself into the task with my usual customer-pleasing gusto, and only when he asked me which one I liked best, and I saw that his face was rather red, did I realize he wasn't talking about photographic versus illustrated.

Harrods was a masterclass in learning how to navigate difficult people, and Richard taught me how to stay calm and not respond to rudeness. One of my colleagues would flush from the neck up when he was getting irate and there would be a dangerous glint in his eye. We called it the red mist. He'd start saying 'Madam' a lot and infusing the word with great scorn.

On the days I did allow something to get to me I'd usually cry rather than be angry; hot tears of humiliation that it was part of my job to allow people to be unpleasant to me. I did once lose my temper when a man refused to believe that Jamie Oliver's books had been published in the order I said they had. I have no idea why it was that man in particular who got under my skin, but I snapped at him and walked off.

My least favourite customers were the authors, usually self-published, who would ask about their own book as though they wanted to buy it, and then, when you said you didn't have it, try to get you to order a copy in. When you politely declined they'd often become aggressive and demand to see a manager, trying to turn their unsolicited sales call into a customer complaint. It was particularly aggravating if you had a queue of genuine customers waiting behind them.

Authors often came in to sign stock and this became part of my job, too. I had to clear a little table, gather up the books, and flap them open to the title page. Then, after the author wrote their name in each one, I'd fasten a cardboard strip called a belly-band around each book so customers would know they were getting a signed copy. It was very enjoyable, though also a bit stressful as the books would sometimes not arrive or go missing, and it was awful to have to tell a visiting author there was nothing in stock. I loved chatting to them, though, and would try to read the books of everyone who came in.

I was amazed at how ordinary most of them were. Growing up, I had thought of authors as godlike creatures, but now I saw they were not that different from anyone else I'd met, which made me wonder if that meant I might be able to become one myself. Often author visits would light up my day. When you are used to getting bossed around on the shop floor, there is an incredible warming bliss in being treated like a human. I still gratefully remember the supportive loveliness of Adele Parks, Kathleen Tessaro, Freya North and

Charlotte Mendelson. Jeffrey Archer came in to sign his prison diaries, and was very jolly and unfazed when a woman walking past said loudly to her friend, 'Look, it's that Jeffrey Archer. I can't stand him.'

We sometimes hosted big author events, and my first of these jobs was looking after the queue of people who had come to meet Bill Wyman. I had to write their name on a Post-it note if they wanted their book signed and dedicated, and generally keep everyone company as we waited. I liked asking people where they'd come from. They were mainly women, very giggly, and all said that Bill Wyman was shorter than they'd expected.

That summer the events manager left and I took over his role. On the days when things went well I felt like a magnificent plate-spinning genius, and when things went wrong it was as though everyone was throwing stones at me from different directions. And so much could go wrong! It was an unpredictable business. If too few people turned up, it was awful for the author to sit there surrounded by piles of books that no one wanted to buy. But if the event was well attended it could quickly become overwhelming, as customers would get restive if they didn't know how or where to queue, or what they were supposed to do.

My pub experience was invaluable. I learnt that you had to prepare for a brief period of intensity and get enough staff in for events as you would for a busy night. Most customers didn't mind waiting if they felt confident that everything was in hand.

I was plagued with anxiety dreams where I'd failed to proofread the posters properly or not ordered the stock in time. The night before John Simpson came in, I dreamt I walked into the unpacking room to find Kate Adie sitting on an enormous pile of boxes, looking down at me. 'You've got the wrong bloody books,' she said.

One of my favourite responsibilities at Harrods was having to guard the delivery of *Harry Potter and the Order of the Phoenix*. The books were under strict embargo, so when two pallets full of boxes were delivered to one of the back-of-house areas, I had to make sure they remained unopened until the end of the day. It was odd to have a period of enforced inactivity. As I sat and looked at the piles I considered my Harry Potter journey, from my first hungover read the day after my twenty-seventh birthday, to queuing up in New York for *The Goblet of Fire*, to becoming the guardian of the pallets. We weren't even allowed to unpack them when the shop was empty but had to come in early the next morning. Having finally seized my copy, I greedily read during my breaks and that evening when I got home. I turned the last page on Sunday morning, sobbing in a greasy spoon near Earl's Court tube, before going back into work to tell my customers how wonderful it was. 'I won't tell you what happens,' I said to them. 'But you can tell from my eyes how much I cried.'

A huge perk of the job was that we would be invited by publishers to launch parties where there was loads of free booze, and sometimes even canapés. Because the pay was so low, lots of us would run out of money by the end of the month, so a well-timed launch was a massive bonus. I'd often get too drunk because I'd been choosing to buy fags rather than food as I eked out the time to payday. The luxury of it could go to your head after a day of being at everyone's beck and call on the shop floor. At a launch for Candace Bushnell's new book, waiters were handing around miniature bottles of pink champagne to be drunk through a straw. I'm ashamed to say I had far more than my fair share and fell down the stairs in the fancy Knightsbridge venue.

Sometimes there were dinners where a publisher would invite booksellers and press to meet an author. I had to brush up on my manners. One night at a dinner at Elena's L'Etoile on Charlotte Street, I was tucking in with great gusto when I noticed that everyone else who already had their food in front of them was waiting for the rest of the table to be served. After that, no matter how knackered and hungry I felt, I trained myself to hold back and observe. If I was confused about which glass or side plate to use then all I had to do was wait and someone else would show me the way.

It was odd to be doing such a menial job during the day yet meeting authors in fine places at night. One author said to me, 'You work for Waterstones?' and I said, 'Well, I work at a branch of Waterstones.'

Another author asked me, 'Are you one of those frightfully important people who decides whether or not my book gets a three-for-two sticker?'

'No,' I said, 'I'm one of those frightfully unimportant people who puts the stickers on, and then has to peel them off again when the books don't sell and they need to be returned.' She looked a bit affronted, and I later twigged I'd been rather clumsy and tactless to suggest her book might not do well. But alas, most books didn't. It could be disheartening to see behind the scenes, to know that for every book that caught the public imagination and flew off the shelves, there were lots more that sold in single digits, and after an all too brief time in the sun – in a little pile on a three-for-two table – would have to be collected, de-stickered and sent back.

As I spent more time with authors I saw that, rather than being cocooned in a blissful bubble of joy because they were published authors, they were often insecure and nervous. Not always, though. Once, at a very boozy launch party, I asked the man next to me not to keep putting his hand up my skirt. 'But I'm an author,' he said, as though that should have granted him access. I can't remember what I replied. As a barmaid, unwanted attention had been an occupational hazard, but I encountered that sort of thing far less frequently in bookish circles. As a woman of my time, I'd been taught to brush it off and find it funny unless the man was aggressive. Now it seems odd to me, the extent to which I accepted such behaviour as the price of being female.

I was unhappy in love all the time I worked at Harrods. For a while I was in a messy relationship where we never seemed to be keen on each other at the same time. One day I was reading *The Colour of Heaven* by James Runcie, in which one of the characters asks another whose voice they would want to hear if they were dying. I was struck by the notion that I most definitely would not want to hear the voice of the man I was currently knocking around with, or even if I did, he might be off somewhere else, not available to soothe me in my final moments because he was too busy trying to chat up one of my friends. So I ended it.

I would love to tell you it was a good clean break and I went off and found some nice person whose voice I did want to hear while I was dying, but alas that was not the case and the on-off mess continued. A couple of years later, I went to see *Private Lives* by Noël Coward, in which Elyot and Amanda can't live with or without each other, and was reminded of the way a passionate reconciliation can turn toxic in the blink of an eye when a chance comment reminds one of you of some previous misdemeanour.

I liked reading novels about the awfulness of romantic love. *Intimacy* by Hanif Kureishi is a book so gloomy about long-term relationships that it cheered me up about being single. In *Intimacy*, teaching English as a foreign language is described as 'the last refuge of the directionless'. A number of booksellers I knew aspired to do TEFL, and one of our more assertive colleagues had just left to do exactly that. I'd considered it myself, after a day of wrangling more than usually difficult customers, but had been too insecure about my grammar to apply. Perhaps the real last refuge of the directionless was bookselling.

I tried writing a novel with a bookseller heroine who embarked on a disastrous relationship with an author after meeting him at a stock signing – I'll leave it up to you, dear reader, to ponder if it might have been inspired by true events – but I was usually too exhausted by bookselling to be able to write about it. I still had loads of notebooks under my bed that I'd been carting around with me for years, and one day in a fit of self-loathing I threw them into a skip. No more trying to write; I would concentrate on enjoying other people's books. I looked forward to the *Bookseller* magazine arriving on Fridays, and I'd take it to read on my breaks so I could be up to date on what was coming out. Even my pleasure in this was dinted when one of my colleagues complained that it always smelled of fags because I read it in the staff smoking room, and from then I was barred from removing it from the shop floor.

I worked at Harrods for nearly two years. Left to my own devices, I doubt I would ever have left. Maybe in a parallel universe I am still there at the front desk, recommending new fiction, answering questions about the toilets and Princess Diana, and pointing people in the direction of Christmas World or the pet shop. I was still very low in confidence and the thought of having to fill out application forms for other jobs filled me with debilitating despair, but one day our regional manager came in, admired my displays, and told me a big new flagship Waterstones was opening on Oxford Street. You should apply, he said. And I did.

Books about Bookshops and Booksellers

I loved books about bookshops long before I got a job in one, and then I loved them even more, though they tend not to be realistic about how hard it is, and characters usually have much more time to loaf about and live an imaginative interior life than a real bookseller does.

The Bookshop by Penelope Fitzgerald
When Florence Green's husband dies, she decides to use her legacy to open a bookshop, and buys a building called the Old House in a small coastal town in Suffolk that hasn't had a bookshop for a hundred years. Florence opens her doors with enthusiasm, but she has unwittingly got on the wrong side of a local bigwig and life gets more and more difficult. Fitzgerald is highly perceptive about human pettiness.

The Thirteenth Tale by Diane Setterfield
'My gripe is not with lovers of the truth but with truth herself. What succour, what consolation is there in truth, compared to a story?' Margaret Lea is a biographer who

lives above her father's antiquarian bookshop. She comes home one day to find a letter from the famous and reclusive writer Vida Winter, who has written a novel every year for the past fifty-six years but has always repelled biographers. As Margaret considers the invitation she wonders why Vida Winter should finally want to tell the truth, and – even curiouser – why she should have chosen Margaret to tell it to.

Business as Usual by Jane Oliver and Ann Stafford
First published in 1933, this story of Hilary Fane's attempts to support herself in London is told through letters home and the departmental memos that are sent about her when she manages to get a job in a department store. Hilary is resilient at enduring the disapproval of her fiancé, the frostiness of her new colleagues, and the difficulties of trying to live on two pounds ten a week. Completely charming and full of wonderful social history about shopping and circulation libraries.

The Shadow of the Wind by Carlos Ruiz Zafón
Daniel's father owns a bookshop in Barcelona. Not long after the end of the Spanish Civil War, he takes Daniel to an enormous library called the Cemetery of Forgotten Books and bids him choose one book and pledge to look after it for his whole life. Daniel chooses *The Shadow of*

the Wind by Julián Carax, and this sets him off on an adventure to find out everything about the mysterious author. Who was he, why did he disappear, and why is there another man intent on destroying his work?

Mr Penumbra's 24-Hour Bookstore by Robin Sloan
When recession and serendipity combine to place web designer Clay Jannon behind the counter at Mr Penumbra's 24-Hour Bookstore, he soon realizes that something strange is afoot. He works the long, lonely night shift where there aren't many customers and those that do come in don't buy anything. What could be going on? As he investigates, he comes up against the biggest questions about human knowledge.

You by Caroline Kepnes
It's 10.06 a.m. on a Tuesday when Guinevere Beck walks into a bookshop in the East Village and heads to Fiction F–K. She's cute and buys the right type of books, and the bookseller, Joe, is smitten. As Joe uses social media to find out about her and insinuates himself into her life, it soon becomes clear that this is no sweet love story. I have never met a more likeable literary psychopath – perhaps I just find it really hard to dislike booksellers!

Enter an Unlikely Hero

Waterstones Oxford Street was a huge shop over three floors, and I loved having so much to learn and so many interesting new colleagues to learn from. The customers were different from those at Harrods, less affluent, and the job was much more about selling bulk copies of the currently popular paperbacks than piling up brand-new hardbacks. Big metal cages of shrink-wrapped stock would come down in the lift and need to be unwrapped, stickered and put out on the shop floor. I learnt a new skill that hadn't been allowed at Harrods: building books into giant floor stacks which would sit ready to replenish the shelves. I found it a very soothing job, and spent many happy moments building enormous towers of *Small Island* by Andrea Levy and *A Short History of Tractors in Ukrainian* by Marina Lewycka.

The joy of a big bookshop is that there is plenty of space for themed displays. I made one of my best ever displays at Oxford Street, based on *1001 Books You Must Read Before You Die*, which I spread across the top of the bay. I chose my favourite books featured inside, and all I put on the recommends cards was the page number where they were written about, so people could discover each one for themselves.

Because the shop was so massive, we would often not be able to find something that should have been in stock. We were trialling kiosks where customers could look up a book and then get a printed slip that would tell them where to find it. This rarely went smoothly and bemused people would wander around like zombies with their slip in an outstretched hand. Even if they did manage to locate True Crime or Painful Lives, and figure out how the books were shelved – A to Z by subject, rather than by author – there was still no guarantee the book would be there.

'But I don't understand,' they would wail. 'The computer says it's in stock. Where can it be?'

As I looked for it, I'd explain, 'I'm so sorry, but the thing with books is, it's really difficult to tell if they are out of place. Someone might have stolen it or just moved it to another shelf. In a supermarket, if an apple ends up with the oranges then it's easy to spot, but with books it's more like a needle in a haystack.'

Some titles were regularly mis-shelved and you'd have to second guess where to look for them. If *Brick*

Lane by Monica Ali wasn't in Fiction, then you'd find it in London. If *Fingersmith* by Sarah Waters wasn't in Fiction, then it would be either in London or the rather oddly named Lesbian Interest. *The Alchemist* by Paulo Coelho was kept variously in Fiction or Mind, Body and Spirit. *Paris Trance* by Geoff Dyer would sometimes turn up in Travel, and no one ever knew how to shelve his collection of essays called *Yoga for People Who Can't Be Bothered to Do It*, except that it definitely didn't belong in Health with the other books that had yoga in the title. *Fear of Flying* by Erica Jong could often be tracked down in Erotica.

The downside of working at the Oxford Street store was the long opening hours. The early shift started at 8 a.m. – I'd always have had three fags by then – and the late shift finished at 9 p.m., or 10 p.m. on Thursdays. Being the late duty manager was pretty grim; it involved fielding complaints about the toilets – they were only cleaned in the mornings so would be in a revolting condition by the end of the day – and sometimes having to encourage drug addicts out of them at closing time. Once a large poo was discovered on the shop floor, and I had to don a pair of marigolds and deal with it. It looked suspiciously human, but I still like to hope it was left by a dog.

I never minded working weekends, because I preferred the shop busy and it felt like a luxury to have a day off during the week. I'd always had enough of the busyness by Christmas, though. On Boxing Day, as I was going into work early to make sure the sale implementation was done, I noticed ice on the inside of the tube window. The morning was taken up with pointless campaign stuff as people more important than me made me move the humour table – mainly constructed of great piles of *Is It Just Me or Is Everything Shit?* – from the front of the shop to the back and then to the front again. Then we opened the doors and my first customer wanted a refund. As I looked at her receipt I clocked the till number and realized it had been me who'd served her, just a few minutes before we closed on Christmas Eve. Neither of us had had much festive time off from consumerism.

Around that time I read *What Was Lost* by Catherine O'Flynn, a funny and sad novel set in a shopping centre in the Midlands which is brilliant on the dark side of working in retail. Lisa is assistant manager at Your Music. Her boss, the 'gangly, cadaverous' Dave Crawford, has rebranded her as the duty manager, which means she is expected to do the worst shifts. Lisa is on duty for early mornings, late nights, Sundays and bank holidays – the times when customers are at their worst and staff are most resentful about having to work.

I'd sit in the staffroom and read out bits to my colleagues about how Crawford would become increasingly manic and paranoid during visits from senior management eager to point out 'missed sales opportunities, sloppy merchandising, woeful lack of product knowledge, poor customer service, chewing gum on the carpet, overly pierced staff.'

Lisa notes how his language becomes more 'macho and violent' the more effete the topic he is enraged about: 'What cunt scuffed this fucking fascia?' This enabled me to giggle silently when one of my superiors interrupted me while I was with a customer to fiercely whisper, 'Get someone to price up the gift wrap as a priority and sort out that calendar stand, it's a fucking disgrace.'

Every six weeks or so, the point of sale material, all the posters and shelf strips, would need to be changed from New Year New You to Valentine's Day, to Mother's Day, to Summer Reading, to Back to School, to Early Gifting, to Christmas, to Sale. It was a fiddly and time-consuming affair, and often the delivery quantities would be wrong. Anyone who was remotely in charge would be stressed out – with good cause, because although the outside world couldn't give a toss about what colour the posters were, the internal drivers were about making sure the campaign 'landed well'. This would be discussed at length and with great seriousness by everyone involved.

Once, a newly recruited regional manager came to our shop to look around.

'What would you do to improve customer service?' he asked me. I was rather excited. No one had ever asked my opinion about anything like this before.

'I don't think store managers should be having nervous breakdowns because table headers haven't arrived,' I said. 'It's bad for staff morale, and the customers get ignored while we run around like headless chickens looking for missing shelf strips.'

He looked at me as though I was insane. 'I think it's very dangerous to suggest that campaign implementation isn't a priority,' he said, and strode off.

Then there was the hideous business of the staff uniform. Some bigwig had decided that booksellers should wear a branded black T-shirt and no one was happy about it. We didn't want to feel like we worked in a garage or a supermarket. It was part of my job to collate sizes from other people and almost everyone was outraged. The back and forth went on and on, and I remember getting to the point where I said, 'I'd wear the fucking thing in bed if it meant I never had to have another conversation about it.' For the first time I felt a bit ashamed of the menial nature of my job, and when an ex-boyfriend came into the shop and said, 'Nice T-shirt' with a smirk, I did feel reduced to a shelf-stacker. At around that time we got a new boss who had never worked in books before, and wanted to rebrand us as 'sales assistants' rather than 'booksellers'. No one liked that either.

I was giving online dating a try and the dates were sometimes fun but often awful. I had to set up a Valentine's display at work, and it was sad to have to collect piles of poetry and love letters and copies of *Pride and Prejudice*, and arrange them nicely while feeling so miserable. Then it occurred to me that I wouldn't be alone in feeling grumpy about love, so I made an antidote – a display to cheer up single people by showcasing how often and how terribly relationships can go wrong. In *A History of the World in 10½ Chapters*, Julian Barnes writes: 'poets seem to be able to turn bad love – selfish, shitty love – into good love poetry. Prose writers lack this power of admirable, dishonest transformation. We can only turn bad love into prose about bad love.' Barnes could single-handedly fill a dumpbin on this theme, but I included lots of other authors and was pleased with my display which prompted funny chats with customers who told me their own romantic horror stories.

I was leaving the shop after work on Valentine's Day when I bumped into Erwyn, the back-of-house manager, near Bond Street tube. 'No date either?' I said. 'Fancy a pint?'

We sat at a table in the Spread Eagle and talked about work. I didn't know Erwyn very well. He was a quiet, unassuming sort of person, and I'd always been impressed by how hard he worked and how much he knew. He was Dutch, and had studied bookselling at college and worked at the Waterstones in Amsterdam. He was from Edam. 'Home of the cheese?' I asked. He told me that tourists came from far and wide to watch it being delivered into the town on canal boat by people dressed in traditional costume. There was no red wax on the cheese in Holland, he said; the red was only for exports.

A girl at a nearby table was crying over a bouquet of red roses. She asked me for a cigarette, and when she left she gave me one of her roses. I tried to get Erwyn interested in what her story might have been but he didn't seem that bothered. We had a few more pints and agreed we'd look suspicious if anyone else from work came in and saw us sitting together on Valentine's Day with a red rose on the table.

Now, knowing the end of the story, it is tempting to believe I saw some significance in this evening, but there was honestly not a frisson or a hint of anything. I did find Erwyn interesting to look at. He had snaggly teeth and one eye that was a different colour from the other, but ever since reading Catherine Cookson I'd had a fondness for physical quirks and was always drawn to scars or mallen streaks or missing fingers, and never put off by imperfection.

I spent Easter Sunday with the people from work who had no other plans. We called ourselves the waifs and strays. Everyone got very drunk, and Erwyn and I ended up together. And carried on being together. And remain so today. I still admire his work ethic and have yet to interest him when I want to make up stories about sad-looking strangers in pubs and restaurants.

I did quite a bit of book buying at Oxford Street. I'd sit down with a rep and they would show me what the publisher had to offer so I could decide whether to order copies for the shop. One day the Penguin rep showed me a new Penguin Modern Classics edition of *Moon Tiger* by Penelope Lively. It was beautiful. It showed Claudia, the red-haired heroine, lying on a bed as the moon tiger, a green coil which repels mosquitos, burns in the corner, gradually doing its work and becoming ash in the process. I was only ever supposed to order one copy of reissued books but, goggle-eyed with desire, I splashed out on sixteen.

Erwyn was in charge of reviewing the subs and came to find me. 'Did you order sixteen copies of a reissue of *Moon Tiger*?'

'Yes,' I squeaked. 'It's one of my favourite books of all time. It has an amazing new cover.'

'Well, you'd better make sure they sell.'

Dear reader, I did.

I was in charge of events, too. We did big signings rather than intimate 'in conversations' so were mainly dealing with celebrities, and the occasional literary author who was big enough to merit the same set-up. Over the course of eighteen months I was enthralled by Zadie Smith, screamed at by Sharon Osbourne, smiled at by David Beckham, hugged by Tracey Emin, had a fag with Ewan McGregor, and was offered sex by Rik Mayall. I think he was joking. I learnt that while most authors are surprisingly normal, lots of celebrities are deeply bizarre, to the extent it must be fame itself that corrodes. Sportspeople tended to be easy to deal with as they were hardworking, disciplined and down to earth. My least favourite subset of famous people were the comedians, who seemed to make it a point of principle not to allow anyone to experience any kind of enjoyment in their presence for free. Chefs were a mixed bag, often vain and competitive and wanting to be reassured that their book was selling better than that of a rival. But they were never fazed by the physical challenge of having to sign hundreds of books.

I learnt that most famous people are smaller than you'd think, except David Hasselhoff who is about eight feet tall. Katie Price was sweet and good-natured, even when her skirt fell off and we had to get safety pins from John Lewis before she could carry on. My worst ever day was when Pelé suddenly had enough and walked off, leaving us with a couple of hundred unhappy customers who'd been queuing for hours. Because of the Sunday trading law we couldn't refund their unsigned books. It was a nightmare. But the evening Zadie Smith signed a copy of *On Beauty* for me and wrote, 'Thank you for showing me the secrets of backstage' was beautiful. And the afternoon that Lauren Bacall – tired and bored – wanted to dwell longer in that same backstage area and asked me to explain goods-in to her while we both sat on kick stools is something I will remember for the rest of my life.

As the launch of *Harry Potter and the Half-Blood Prince* approached, I was given some media training so I could talk to the press. I found it very stimulating and it was great fun to be on the TV and radio that night. We had nearly two thousand customers through the shop in less than three hours and it was exhilarating, though I lifted a crash barrier and did something to my lower back that has never healed. Doing press was a whole new level of talking to strangers about books and I loved it. In the following months I was interviewed about the shop for the *Bookseller* and the *Guardian*, appeared on a documentary about Georgette Heyer, and was asked to recommend a book for a slot on a short-lived arts programme. I talked about *Moon Tiger*. 'You're really good at this,' said the producer. 'You should do more of it.' How? I wanted to scream. How? Though I didn't even dare to ask. I was too shy and ashamed to admit my desires.

That Christmas I did a secondment where I looked after events at both Oxford Street and the flagship shop at Piccadilly. The building was massive and the lift would often break, making it difficult to transport stock – or wine and mince pies for the Christmas customer evening – around the building. By the New Year I was exhausted. I had completely lost my voice and had had to leave the room during our event with Ian Rankin because I couldn't stop coughing. He was very nice about having to introduce himself.

Although I loved the excitement, I'd grown tired of some of the customers who came to celebrity events, who were often so fixated on meeting the famous person in question that they would try anything to get what they wanted. Some people who queued up to see Paul Mc-Cartney or U2 were convinced that they were destined to be best friends with their idol if only the boring intermediaries like me could be got out of the way. I felt bruised when an obnoxious woman managed to get a free signed copy by untruthfully complaining about me to my boss. I cried myself to sleep that night, distraught that I was in my thirties, working so hard for so little money, and still in thrall to anyone who fancied making my life just that tiny bit harder. I looked at other jobs but balked at the application forms again and never managed to complete one.

One day at work I wandered into the self-help section in the basement. I was inclined to turn my nose up and feel a bit sorry for sad-eyed women buying *The Rules*, but I wanted to have a look at some of the books about jobs. One of them had a line on the cover that said, 'Why not consider a portfolio career?' I stood there in my branded T-shirt, sneaking a quick read before some customer would interrupt to bend me to their will, and thought, How the fuck does someone like me get a portfolio career? I felt so stuck. My grief for Matty was never far away, and would rear up and threaten to overwhelm me without warning. I had locked it away, though. After years of drunkenly crying to anyone who would listen, I'd learnt that no one really wanted to know and so I kept my sadness hugged to myself.

Life jogged along. My parents took Erwyn and me to Paris for the weekend. I loved the lock-up stalls by the Seine where people sold art, and I fantasized over having my own book version. I'd carry no range, just have ten or twelve favourite books at any time and press them on passers-by who looked in need of a good read. We stumbled across an English bookshop called The Red

Wheelbarrow and I bought a copy of *Moon Tiger* for my mum. I got chatting about bookselling to the owner at the desk. 'If you ever want a job . . .' she said.

Part of me was hugely tempted. Why couldn't this have happened before I met Erwyn? I felt the same as I perused the internal jobs bulletin when I got back to work. Cork! I could live in the city where my father was born and spend more time with my Irish family. Then I heard that Hatchards needed an assistant manager. I had loved that shop since reading about it in Mary Wesley novels all those years ago. And there was no staff uniform! I enjoyed my interview with the man who became my new boss. He bumped into Erwyn a couple of days later and said, 'She's brilliant, but quite mad.'

'A bit eccentric, maybe,' said Erwyn.

My last event at Waterstones Oxford Street was Kylie Minogue – tiny and delightful – on Erwyn's thirtieth birthday. There is now a Uniqlo on the site where the shop used to be. I walk by it every so often. The last time I was there, I caught a whiff from the hot dog vendor which catapulted me right back to the after-work pints at the Duke of York or the Cock Tavern, and late nights at the Spanish bar on Hanway Street. I remembered when Dr Gillian McKeith came to do an event for *You Are What You Eat*, and I joked in the staffroom that if she was right, what I most resembled was a pint of lager with a couple of fag ends floating on the top and a half-eaten hot dog on the side.

It's the camaraderie and the jokes that stay with me. We had a large erotica section and a recommends card saying, 'This one really got me going' that we would move around to put under random books. That made me laugh every time I walked by it and still gives me a smile.

Looking through some boxes of stuff before our house move, I found my leaving card, full of lovely messages from my colleagues. Erwyn had written: 'Good luck at Hatchards. I'm glad I'll still get to see you every day.'

Bad Love

It is a truth universally acknowledged that love is more interesting and worthy of being written about when it goes wrong. If you meet a happily married couple at the beginning of a novel, you know they won't be staying that way. Either one of them will be lying to the other – or they will both be lying to everyone. Deceit, adultery, obsession and betrayal work brilliantly in fiction, and some of the best novels are about the despair and disillusion caused by matters of the heart.

Talking It Over/Love, Etc by Julian Barnes

In *Talking It Over*, Stuart, Oliver and Gillian – the three points of a love triangle – offer their accounts of how Gillian started out being married to Stuart and ended up with Oliver. In *Love, Etc* we revisit them a decade later to see how things have changed. Because the story hasn't ended, Stuart tells us. Maybe he wishes it had, 'But life never lets you go, does it? You can't put life down the way you can put a book down.'

Heartburn by Nora Ephron

Nora Ephron was seven months pregnant with her second child when she found out that her husband was having an affair with a mutual friend. Her mother had always told her 'everything is copy' so she turned it into a brilliant comic novel. The edition I often reread comes with a wonderful introduction written twenty-two years later: 'I knew the moment my marriage ended that someday it might make a book – if I could just stop crying.'

What Belongs to You by Garth Greenwell

When an American teacher meets a young man called Mitko in the toilets of the National Palace of Culture in Sofia, he becomes obsessed with his desire for him. A slender and achingly beautiful novel full of the gloriously messy pain of unrequited and inappropriate love. A little like *Of Human Bondage* by W. Somerset Maugham, it captures the terrible truth that knowing the object of our love is unworthy does not help us to stop pining for their attention.

The End of the Affair by Graham Greene

'The sense of unhappiness is so much easier to convey than that of happiness.' The love affair between Maurice Bendrix and Sarah Miles comes to an end after a bomb falls on his flat just after they have made love. Bendrix doesn't understand why Sarah won't see him any more and descends into bitter jealousy. Two years later, he runs into Sarah's husband and becomes tangled up again in his obsessive love for a woman he doesn't understand.

Apple Tree Yard by Louise Doughty
Respected scientist Yvonne Carmichael steps out of giving evidence to a House of Commons Select Committee and into the path of a man she finds dangerously attractive. Without considering the consequences, she has sex with him in the Chapel in the Crypt, and so begins an affair that will lead her to the dock at the Old Bailey and to the last in a long line of betrayals. I love this portrait of a woman unravelling, the geographical details of London, and the way the significance of Apple Tree Yard is revealed.

A Little Life by Hanya Yanagihara
Jude, JB, Willem and Malcolm are making their way in New York City. What starts off feeling like a fairly traditional post-college novel takes a darker turn as we gradually discover the secrets in Jude's past that prevent him from fully living in the present. I won't lie to you, dear reader: there is little comfort or joy in this novel, but it is a work of genius that asks the hardest questions about the limitations of love.

Black Monday

Hatchards is the oldest bookshop in England – it was established by John Hatchard in 1797 – and sits on Piccadilly next door to Fortnum & Mason. Many of our customers would come up from the country to visit both shops and then have lunch. As I'd imagined, they were like characters straight out of a Mary Wesley novel and I loved observing them. They were usually polite, much more so than the customers at Harrods, and the good people of Oxford Street, who were harried and hurried and often shopping on a rushed break from work. Hatchards customers were pleasant and, providing you knew your stuff, which I did, appreciative. They were often rather elderly, and I got used to having my recommendations turned down because the font was too small. I loved them, these posh, old people, and used to yearn to be the grandchild for whom they were buying presents.

Some of the men would say, 'I don't read books written by women,' but I'd often manage to get something onto their pile by enthusing about it at length and then saying, 'Oh, but it *is* written by a woman,' and making to put it back on the table. Appetite firmly whetted, they'd snatch it from me, and so I changed the reading habits of a fair few men during my time there. One of my favourite moments was up in Military History, where I had a long chat with a tweedy old man buying a book about D-Day who said, 'You know a lot about war, for a woman.'

The hours were more civilized, too, as we closed at 7 p.m. It was a very old building with one lift that regularly broke down, so I spent a lot of time running up and down the stairs for the customers with walking sticks, which was wearying when the temperamental air conditioning went on the blink and the shop became increasingly cauldron-like. I'd been on a management training course that had included a bit about how to cope when things went wrong. The idea was to work out what was in your control and focus on that. I applied what I'd learnt one hot Saturday. 'Well,' I said to myself, 'I can't control the fact that the lift has broken, and the aircon isn't working, and three people have phoned in sick, but I can control my own reaction to it.'

Sometimes the power would cut out. Back in the mists of time, the shop had been two buildings, and we were wired on different grids so could find ourselves with lights but no computers. I rather liked it when the systems went down and we had to rely on the information in our heads. Once, when the basement went dark, we had to evacuate the customers and a man in the erotica section refused to leave. Eventually I left him to it and he was still there when the lights went back on an hour later.

I spent much of my time serving at the front desk. Many customers bought *Slipstream*, the recently published memoir in which Elizabeth Jane Howard described her extremely novelistic life; her wartime marriage to Sir Peter Scott and her numerous affairs and subsequent second marriage, before meeting Kingsley Amis at Cheltenham Literature Festival and eventually marrying him.

I read *Slipstream* on my breaks and then dived into the Cazalet Chronicles, where I found that Howard had already explored a lot of her autobiographical material by gifting her life events to her characters. The series of novels starts with *The Light Years*, which opens in 1937 as the various members of the Cazalet family have differing opinions on just how dangerous Hitler might turn out to be. The Cazalet brothers work in the family timber firm and their wives have varying attitudes towards sex. Villy finds it a chore that Edward wants to lift up her nightdress so often, but her mother told her never to refuse so she has cultivated an attitude of patient distaste and thinks of it as a way to prove her love. Sybil adores Hugh and longs to soothe the headaches and pains that, along with an amputated hand, are his wartime legacy, but worries about becoming pregnant again. Rupert's wife Zoë, who has plenty of SA, as the others say, is spoilt, but then we find out her father died at the Somme and she was sent to boarding school at the age of five, so that her mother could take a job with Elizabeth Arden doing women's faces all day. Zoë is reading *Gone with the Wind*, enjoying the passionate scenes. It is suggested that Zoë, like Scarlett O'Hara, is 'as shallow as a soup bowl'.

War looms. The effects of the first are still felt as the threat of another grows increasingly difficult to ignore. Hugh sees that it is a mistake to write Hitler off as absurd or mad, and worries about Chamberlain, who does not strike him as a leader who would be much good at getting people's heads out of the sand.

Each time I revisit the Cazalet Chronicles, I greedily hoover up the domestic details and can almost taste the food: hot boiled gammon with parsley sauce and broad beans, Charlotte Russe, treacle tart, Terry's bitter chocolate, hot Bovril on the beach, kidneys for breakfast, sheep's brains wrapped up in greaseproof paper. People drink and smoke a lot – much of the action happens with a dry martini in one hand and a gasper in the other.

The lives of the servants and their employers are contrasted to great effect. The ladies wear diamond arrows;
the servants wear straw hats. When the women have
their periods they go to the linen cupboard for flannel,
which they fold into strips. The dirty bags get sent to the
laundry labelled 'sanitary napkins'. There is a different
bag for the servants and the ladies of the house.

The Cazalet women we meet as children in *The Light
Years* – Louise, Polly and Clary – are creative and artistic,
so often end up in thrall to the wrong sort of man, as did
Howard herself. Laurie Lee told her that no one as pretty
as she was would be able to write well. Arthur Koestler
liked her to shut up and eat her dinner. Kingsley Amis,
when he eventually got round to reading one of her novels,
was relieved and surprised to find that it was any good.
Howard didn't write much when she was shacked up with
Amis, pouring his drinks and looking after his kids. Later,
in an interview, she said that 'Kingsley wasn't one to boil an
egg,' which might be the best seven-word sentence ever.
I liked to read about these young women as I pondered
my own disastrous love affairs, which now seemed safely
in the past as I was happy with my tall, shy Dutchman.

One of the habits I developed while working at
Hatchards was to have a reading project on the go. This
started as a New Year's resolution to read the twelve
novels that make up *A Dance to the Music of Time* by

Anthony Powell – my diary from the time says, 'Glad I've done it, but also glad it's over.' I enjoyed the notion so much I decided it was a shame to confine it to January, and immediately started working through the ten novels of *Alms for Oblivion* by Simon Raven – 'very, very good' – and then John Galsworthy's *The Forsyte Saga* before being defeated by Proust.

Lots of authors came into Hatchards to sign stock, and we had a pretty little half-moon table for the purpose. There was an annual Author of the Year party where the guests would sign their names in a beautiful leather-bound book. Often, as I shelved, I would make up historical crime novels in my head, where an author would be murdered during the party and the bookseller heroine – who was rather like me – would have to join forces with a detective to figure it out.

One of the best places to be was down in the basement with the paperback fiction. I would soothe myself by putting the Georgette Heyers into alphabetical order and recommending them to visiting Americans who wanted something especially English. They have the comfort of escapism with a lovely dollop of well-researched history and plenty of humour. Georgette Heyer said of her own books: 'I think myself I ought to be shot for writing such nonsense, but it's unquestionably good escapist literature; and I think I should rather like it if I were sitting in an air-raid shelter, or recovering from flu.' She also wrote a few crime novels and they were reissued when I was at Hatchards, so they went into our delightful classic crime section. The books are often funny. Georgette Heyer would not have known the term 'mansplaining' but her novels are full of patronizing and overbearing men who think they know best, as well her charming, often rakish heroes.

I was sorely in need of good escapist literature around that time. One Monday in January 2007, Erwyn and I went to hospital for my pregnancy scan. We were hugely excited. My mother had a hospital appointment that same day down in Cornwall, to have a cyst under her arm looked at. She wasn't worried. She'd had several before and they'd been benign.

There's that moment, when you are lying there with gel all over your tummy and you realize that the sonographer is bracing herself to deliver bad news. We stumbled out of the hospital and Erwyn held me as I cried sitting on the wall by the bus stop. When I got home I phoned my mum. Dad answered. Mum's appointment was taking longer than they'd expected. I told him about the miscarriage. 'It's normal,' I said, passing on what I'd learnt from the sonographer. 'It happens a lot in early pregnancy.' I went to bed for the afternoon and sobbed into my pillow for my little lost baby. Time ticked on. I phoned my mum. Dad answered again. 'We'll call you when she gets out,' he said.

Mum rang in the early evening. She asked me about what had happened at the hospital and I told her. Then she said, 'Well, I've got some difficult news.' She'd spent the day having various scans and they were 95 per cent sure she had breast cancer. I felt like the breath had been crushed out of me. I'd thought I was already as sad as I could be, and it was disorienting to plummet to a new level. Mum explained everything that would happen next: more scans, appointments, biopsies. She was calm. I was crying. 'You know,' she said, 'the prognosis isn't bad for breast cancer. And I was thinking today that if this is it, then at least it's happening when you are thirty-five, not two, or five, or ten. At least we've had thirty-five years together.'

My boss at Hatchards was extremely supportive, and over the next few months I arranged my shifts so that I could work intensively and then get the sleeper train down to Cornwall, spend a couple of days with my parents, accompany my mum to chemo, and then get the sleeper train back to London and head straight into work. It was often sad and hard, and we were frightened, but we'd decided to try to get as much joy out of being together as we could. There were laughs to be had over the wigs, which Mum thought made her look rather too smart and coiffed to be realistic. She settled for a collection of jaunty nautical headscarves instead. She was very funny about the fact that people kept complimenting her on her positive attitude. 'What I don't understand, if I'm so positive, is how did I get the cancer in the first place?'

She didn't want to see many people. The chemo made her feel like she was poisonous, even contagious. Later she would throw away everything associated with it.

On my parents' bookshelves was a big blue hardback of Daphne du Maurier's Cornish novels, and I'd read a different one each time I went down. Dad was reading more, too. I'd given him a signed David Beckham autobiography after our Oxford Street event with him. I hadn't expected him to read it, but he was proud of my job and admired David Beckham so I thought he'd like to own a copy. To my surprise he had tucked in, then moved on to other sports biographies before starting on thrillers.

He wanted to read a classic so I rummaged around the shelves and found a copy of *Jane Eyre*. The next time I visited I asked how he was getting on. He looked sad and ashamed and told me he couldn't make sense of it. I was surprised. I'd chosen *Jane Eyre* because I thought the opening was readable and easy to grasp. I picked the book up from the table and found that, because it was one of my university books, there was a chunky, scholarly introduction. Dad wasn't a reader, so didn't know that he could choose to skip it. No wonder he'd been having such a difficult time.

Over the next few weeks he carried on reading my recommendations. He was inclined to think that if he didn't like something it was his fault, that he was too stupid for it. 'Think of it like TV or songs,' I said, 'you're allowed not to like things. Not everything will be up your street.' To my surprise, he didn't want to read much set in Ireland. He enjoyed *Borstal Boy* and *Confessions of an Irish Rebel* by Brendan Behan because they were funny, but when I gave him other Irish books he found them depressing. He didn't want to read about poverty and horrible priests. He'd had enough of that in his own childhood, he said, and would rather forget it than be reminded of it.

It was a strange switch. All my life I'd been talking about books with my mum, but now she didn't have the attention span for reading. She'd be too ill after chemo to talk on the phone, so Dad would ring me up, tell me she was as well as could be expected, and we'd discuss what he'd been reading. It was exciting to talk to him about books and he often surprised me with his opinions. The very fact he'd had no formal education meant there was an appealing originality to the way he thought. Unlike me with my bookseller mentality, he didn't think to categorize books, so he read *Any Human Heart* by William Boyd thinking it was a real diary rather than a novel. And there was no snobbery about him. It didn't occur to him to judge books on their literary merit. Unlike so many Hatchards customers, he didn't distinguish between male and female authors and would approach each book as its own unique thing. 'People stare at me,' he said that summer, when he was wearing shorts and the green inked dragon that runs down his leg was visible. 'No one expects to see a man with as many tattoos as I've got reading a book.'

Posh People Behaving Badly

I read a lot on those long train journeys, working my way through the 'posh people behaving badly' books that sold so well at Hatchards. Perhaps I loved them for the sheer contrast they offered to my own life, or maybe because they had a joyous 'don't give a fuck' quality. The people in them were often maintaining a stiff upper lip in times of trouble or telling dubious jokes in the face of personal tragedy. At that strange, sad time, it was exactly what I needed.

The Pursuit of Love by Nancy Mitford
Fanny and her many cousins spend their childhood in the Hons' cupboard, talking about life and death. Linda can't wait to be grown up enough to find love, but she chooses badly and ends up sitting sobbing on her suitcase at the Gare du Nord. Enter Fabrice, a rich duke who rescues her and loves her until the war separates them. I discovered Nancy Mitford back in Snaith Library when I read about her in Jilly Cooper's anthology *The British in Love*, and have been enthralled ever since.

Hons and Rebels by Jessica Mitford

Many of Nancy Mitford's novels are based on her childhood with her six siblings, one of whom – Jassy – is always saving up money and will sell her Christmas presents to grow her running away fund. Here, Nancy's sister Jessica tells her side of the story in a memoir that covers her real-life flight when she eloped with her cousin, Esmond, and they ran off together to the Spanish Civil War.

The Duff Cooper Diaries edited by John Julius Norwich

A soldier, politician and diplomat, Duff Cooper had a fondness for fine wine and a weakness for almost any type of woman, which he indulged despite a sincere attachment to his wife, Diana. His observations of the biggest political events of the century are interspersed with an endless stream of flirtations, tumbles and full-blown passions, and the combination of affairs of state with backstairs gossip and philandering is irresistible. I'm fond of this line: 'She was the first unmarried woman I'd kissed, apart from prostitutes.'

Darling Monster by Diana Cooper

Aristocrat and actress and society darling, Lady Diana's marriage to political rising star Duff Cooper positioned them as a couple at the heart of Establishment life in the first half of the twentieth century. These letters from Lady Diana to her son, John Julius Norwich, span from 1939 to 1952, covering the war and Duff's tenure at the British Embassy in Paris, giving another view to the events covered in his diaries. The letters are full of maternal love and scandalous anecdotage.

Mapp and Lucia by E. F. Benson

When Emmeline Lucas, known as Lucia due to her penchant for speaking Italian, moves to Tilling and rents Mallards from Miss Mapp, a battle for social supremacy rages. Miss Mapp tries to monopolize Lucia, but Lucia rebels and courts the good people of Tilling with an irresistible array of bridge evenings, musical recitals and garden parties. How will Mapp get her revenge?

Reader, I Married Him

Erwyn and I got married on Easter Saturday 2009 in a registry office in Richmond, not far from where Virginia Woolf used to live and round the corner from the Mills & Boon offices on Paradise Road. I was six months pregnant with our son Matt and my mum was cancer-free with short, tight, grey curls all over her head. Chemo had taken so much out of her, but she was delighted to be alive and said she woke up every morning happy to have another day.

Almost all the guests who weren't related to us worked at Waterstones. My first husband John was one of our witnesses. I had done a reading at his wedding a few months earlier when he'd married my dear friend Lizzie, who I'd met at Harrods. It was a happy day, surrounded by daffodils. I hadn't known it, but my Aunt Marion told me that my grandparents had married on Easter Saturday, too. Their favourite song was 'Can't

Take My Eyes Off You' by Frankie Valli, and we played it over lunch in the upstairs room of a little restaurant by the river.

By this time, I was the manager at Waterstones Teddington, a lovely little shop that opened from 9 to 5.30 and had lots of regular customers. Because the shop was so small – it would fit three or four times over into one floor at Piccadilly – nothing ever went that badly wrong, though I'd had to get used to operating with fewer titles to hand. At first, I'd start chatting to a customer and end up recommending something we didn't have in stock, but then I put in an order for a few of my favourites so I could always jump on an opportunity to create new lovers of *Moon Tiger* or *Not That Sort of Girl*. Erwyn was working at head office then – he'd got a job in the returns department after the Oxford Street store closed down – so he had weekends free, and would often come in with me and shelve or pick returns. Doing the rota and payroll didn't take long so I could spend most of my time at the front desk – the only desk – with my colleagues and customers, who were delightful. There were no events, no famous people, just the pleasant rhythms of daily life. Even Christmas had been fun and our customers had brought in homemade mince pies.

As I got bigger and bigger, the staff looked after me and the customers would give me advice and pat my bump. I know some women don't like this but I decided to think of it as a benediction, an instinct to offer affection to a new life. I felt at the heart of a community and that everyone was cherishing me and my baby.

My reading habits changed, too. One lunchtime I took a proof of the new Linwood Barclay novel off the trolley. A very short time later I put it back. I could see that a child was about to go missing and knew I wouldn't be able to handle it. It marked the start of a new relationship with crime novels that has never quite gone away. With a baby growing inside me, I could no longer read about children in peril.

Somewhere towards the end of my pregnancy, I lost the desire for reading anything other than childcare manuals and Georgette Heyer and gentle classic crime novels with no gore. I'd potter down to Chiswick Library and sit in the sun on the bench outside, which had a plaque that said, 'For my mother, a woman of courage and compassion.' I reread the Brother Cadfael novels, which are full of these exact qualities, and bought a lovely book called *Becoming a Mother* by Kate Mosse. As I read it in the bath, I watched the movement of my baby under my skin.

Matt obviously liked jumping about in my tummy because my due date came and went and he stayed put. Erwyn said that Edammers are known for being stubborn, and that Matt must be a little *dwarse Edammer*, refusing to come out.

Two weeks later, I was induced. The birth was complicated and ended in an emergency caesarean. Matt needed antibiotics because of my fever and screamed his head off as they put a cannula into his foot. That night as he slept in his clear plastic cot next to my bed, I looked around at the other mothers and babies and felt full of concerned love. How would we cope?

Having a baby tenderized me to the fate of all babies. I had always been a crier but had now become a watering can. The merest hint that a child was in danger or trouble, or even just a bit lonely, would make me sob and sob.

Back at home I kept a diary from Matt's perspective to help me keep track of his naps and feeds: 'I am in my sleeping bag and Mummy and Daddy hope I will settle down in my cot . . . During the night I cried a lot and no one knows why . . . Mummy cried because she couldn't get the breast pump to work . . . Projectile vomited on Mummy . . . The midwife came. I am a healthy baby! . . . John and Lizzie visited me . . . I weed on Daddy as he was changing my nappy and Mummy thought it was hilarious . . .'

I'd looked forward to maternity leave in a way that only someone who has yet to look after a baby can, thinking I'd have time to read and write. Instead my brain turned to mush, and I was so tired and pulled about by the birth that I spent many of my waking hours in tears. I wasn't especially unhappy, it was just so overwhelming. Certainly nothing I'd read had in any way prepared me for the reality of the anguished love and fear that was sloshing around in my battered body. I kept thinking of a David Lodge quote: 'Literature is mostly about having sex and not much about having children. Life is the other way round.' I found a book called *Life After Birth* by Kate Figes that helped me a lot. I wrote in my diary: 'I mustn't feel bad that things aren't perfect. Everything with a baby is bloody hard work and I might as well accept it.'

I was glad to at least have a Christmas off work, but when I pushed Matt's pram around the Waterstones in Chiswick that autumn, I hated that I didn't know the books on the tables and didn't enjoy feeling like a civilian. Perhaps this was the first sign of wanting to read new books again. Matt and I went to the library a lot to do rhyme times and sing-a-longs, and just to get out of the flat. We only ever went to the children's section, but one day as I was getting out some picture books, a copy of *Wolf Hall* by Hilary Mantel caught my eye. It was massive! How would I even hold it? I ran my fingers over it. Was that a tingle I could feel through the plastic cover? I couldn't resist.

I have a photo of Matt at a few months old stretched out over the big hardback. I tried and failed to read it as I was breastfeeding – it was too big to balance – but would pick it up after Matt had fallen asleep on my chest, holding the book aloft and taking care not to drop it onto his tiny head. It hurt my wrists, which were altered by pregnancy, but I was too entranced to stop reading. I remember the profound sense of relief that I could tackle big complex books again. I hadn't felt right before, like I'd been robbed of my magic powers.

Wolf Hall tells a story I was familiar with from those Jean Plaidy and Norah Lofts books, though Mantel makes the familiar into something new, breathing life and vigour into old tales. We see Henry VIII and his need for Anne through the eyes of Thomas Cromwell. In most historical fiction, Cromwell is the villain and Thomas More is the saint, but Mantel flips it so that if you had to choose which Thomas to meet down a dark alley it would be Cromwell every time. He is a widower and a bereaved father and, as Mantel writes him, he seems like a sensible and sympathetic man.

It's an odd book to read as your healthy baby son kicks his legs on a blanket. What wouldn't Henry or Katherine or Anne have done for such a child? When the time draws near for Anne to give birth, she is confined to her rooms in Greenwich, but the much-desired baby is a girl. Cromwell goes to see her: 'The princess, unswaddled, had been placed on cushions at Anne's feet: an ugly, purple, grizzling knot of womankind, with an upstanding ruff of pale hair and a habit of kicking up her gown as if to display her most unfortunate feature.'

Matt liked my voice and it was important for him to hear words, so often I read aloud to him. I didn't read him any of the bits about religious persecution. The more alert he became, the less comfortable I felt reading him adult books, and I stopped doing it altogether a couple of chapters into *Damage* by Josephine Hart. Although he couldn't understand a word, I didn't want to pollute him with too much adult despair. Or maybe it was just that *Damage* didn't suit being read aloud in my baby-pleasing voice.

After that I read kids' books to him. I especially liked ones that rhymed, and *Tiddler* by Julia Donaldson – about a fish with a big imagination – became a huge favourite of us both. I sang a lot, too, and made up a song inspired by those Irish ones my dad used to sing to me, where the narrator always seems to be measuring the distance from one place to another: 'Oh, he is the loveliest baby that the world has ever seen, from Donegal to Kerry and from Cork to Skibbereen.'

We also listened to audiobooks that I got out from the library. I'd read *The Time Traveler's Wife* by Audrey

Niffenegger, which came out when I was working at Harrods, but everything about Henry and Claire wanting a baby meant so much more to me now, and I sobbed my way through it. Another highlight was a memoir by Antonia Fraser called *Must You Go? My Life with Harold Pinter*. It was full of magnificent grandeur intoned in the poshest voice I'd ever heard, with lines like, 'The day I got divorced I went on my own to *La Bohème* and sat in a black velvet cloak and cried my heart and eyes out in the last act.' There were little connections; they met on my second birthday, and had a jolly time in a pub after a cricket match near where we lived. I couldn't imagine a life where Harold Pinter might pop in and read me Larkin in the bath, and giggled over it as I scrubbed the toilet. I bet Antonia Fraser has a cleaner, I thought, and wondered how her life with Harold Pinter would have been affected if she'd had to wipe up his pubes.

Needing something to do while Matt was asleep, I signed up for an Open University creative writing module. I wrote short stories about miscarriages and marriage, both from the perspective of men. For the life-writing assignment I made notes for a piece called 'My Life Without Harold Pinter', in which I intended to explore not having a black velvet cloak or a cleaner or someone who read their play to me in the bath. But in the end I decided it was feeble and dishonest not to write about Matty's death, which still seemed like the most significant thing that had ever happened to me, even though I never spoke about it. I couldn't face it head on, so I wrote about the night of the accident in the third person. I also wrote the first chapter of a novel as my final assignment. I meant to carry on after the course was finished but, liberated from deadlines, I couldn't summon up the will. My maternity leave was drawing to a close and it was time to go back to work.

Mothers and their Children

There is so much written about falling in love that it seems impossible to make an original reflection on the subject. Mothering, however, is less well covered in literature, presumably because women are too caught up in caring for their babies to be writing anything down. These books show us the maternal relationship in all its complexity.

The End We Start From by Megan Hunter
In a future so near it feels like now, our narrator gives birth to her son in a London under threat of advancing flood waters. Because she lives in the 'Gulp Zone' she must head off in search of shelter and safety, but the familiar has become dangerous as social order breaks down. I loved the way the journey into the unfamiliar territory of motherhood is contrasted with the need to move out of danger. And it is fascinating to reimagine London as a place to flee from, its population turned into refugees.

Dept. of Speculation by Jenny Offill
'There is still such crookedness in my heart. I had thought loving two people so much would straighten it.'

In forty-six short chapters, our narrator takes us through the stages of a marriage, from wide-eyed curiosity to resentful whispered fights to uneasy accommodations. The terror and fatigue that comes with being in charge of a newborn is perfectly captured, as is the sadness of waning love and the impossibility of creating art while drowning in domesticity.

My Name is Leon by Kit de Waal
'Leon has begun to notice the things that make his mum cry.' Leon is nearly nine when his little brother Jake is born and instantly adores him, but as their mum fails to cope their little family unit comes under threat. Leon isn't stupid – he doesn't believe in Father Christmas and he knows when adults are doing pretend faces – but it still comes as a shock to find that he might be left behind when Jake is adopted because Jake is white and he is not.

Grief is the Thing with Feathers by Max Porter
'We were small boys with remote-control cars and ink-stamp sets and we knew something was up.' The mother is dead in this sad and funny story, leaving her husband, a Ted Hughes scholar, to look after their two sons. He's not alone for long as a crow descends to offer advice. The boys with their cries of 'We don't want baths, our bums are clean!' are adorable; as is their father, when he

promises to get a bit more teaching work and stop thinking quite so much about Ted Hughes.

The Mother by Yvvette Edwards

Marcia's son Ryan was stabbed to death for no apparent reason, and now she goes to court every day to see if the young man accused of his murder will be convicted. Ryan had never been in trouble so why was he carrying a knife? There are plenty of twists and turns as this courtroom drama unfolds, and through it all the question dominates of what it must be like to lose a son to a violent and unjust death.

The Green Road by Anne Enright

Rosaleen Madigan's children have left her behind in the family home on the west coast of Ireland to travel the world. Now Rosaleen says she is selling the house and wants them to come home for one last Christmas. A magnificent novel about family and belonging – it includes a Christmas shopping scene that makes me howl with laughter.

Working Mum

I returned to work as the manager of the Waterstones in Richmond, a lovely shop near the river. It was physically hard because pregnancy and giving birth had altered my body. My back and wrists were knackered, so simple things like lifting the tills in and out were painful and I couldn't carry more than a few books at a time. I missed the days when I could stride across the shop floor with great piles of paperbacks. Another problem was that I hadn't fully realized the extent to which my working life had depended on doing extra hours. Since Oxford Street I'd accepted that it was part of my job to go in early and leave late, but now that I had to race to the childminder's house to pick Matt up I was supposed to be leaving on the dot. On my first day we caught someone stealing an e-reader, and I couldn't leave halfway through being interviewed by the police. On my second day we had a random fire safety check, and at closing time I was still being told off by the fire officer about the excess furniture in the back-of-house areas.

'What are they, anyway?' he asked.

'Dumpbins,' I said. 'You put books in them.'

'Funny name,' he said.

'You're right,' I said.

My childminder was wonderful and flexible but I had to pay her for extra time. I worked out that after the cost of childcare I was earning £26 per day, and that if I kept being late and needing to pay more, I could end up being out of pocket for the privilege of going to work. I didn't begrudge the money, though. Since having a baby I'd learnt that anyone who works with little ones is certainly earning their pay packet. And there was no question that I wanted to be at work. I was delighted to be having conversations with grown-ups. No matter what happens today, I would think as I walked down Richmond High Street, it is very unlikely that anyone will be sick on me.

There was an electrical shop on the high street that always had an A-frame outside advertising a 'Manager's Special'. Inspired by this, I set up a dumpbin on the ground floor, filled it with my favourite books – nothing new, just tried and tested boon companions – and felt I'd achieved the spirit of what I'd longed for when I looked at the lock-up stalls by the Seine in Paris. I had set out my own little dumpbin of delights, which sat amid the hustle and bustle of new books coming in and out.

The staff at Richmond were hardworking, friendly and knew what they were doing. One of my new colleagues said, 'We're a bit worried you're a high flyer and won't stay very long.' I was amused by this perception of me, as that wasn't how I felt, but could see that I'd come a long way from the time when I couldn't make eye contact at a job interview.

'I don't know how long I'll stay,' I said, 'but I'll care really hard about you while I'm here. That's as much as I can promise.' I did always try to be a good boss, and would often reread passages from *What Was Lost* to remind myself not to get strung out by regional manager or head office visits. I started misquoting Oscar Wilde to jolly us through difficult or pointless tasks: 'We are all in the operational gutter, but the trick is to try to keep sight of the stars.'

Having Matt had focused me on my career in a way I'd never felt before. I worked every Saturday so that I could have a day off in the week to spend with him. One Saturday, Erwyn brought Matt into the shop to say hello just at the moment when a customer was shouting at me, for some reason I have long since forgotten. What I remember is that the angry man was calling me 'young lady' and that his spittle was landing on my face. I'd taught myself to feel proud of my ability to tolerate customer abuse over the years, but something about Matt being within earshot made me feel differently. I didn't want him to grow up watching his mother be mistreated or shouted at by anyone who couldn't control their temper.

I started to want more and different work, though didn't know how to get it. And then I was asked to do a little stint on stage at the Waterstones publisher conference. The other speakers were from head office but they wanted a shop-based person to give another perspective.

I was excited to escape from my daily routine but also nervous. The other presenters had PowerPoint slides with pie charts and statistics. All I had was a book.

My stomach churned as I walked on stage. 'My name is Cathy,' I said, 'and I like talking to strangers about books.' I'd expected to be able to see the faces of people in the audience, but now the stage lighting was on I looked out into endless black. I glanced up at the screen behind me, looking for the picture I'd asked for, of the book that was in my hand: *Moon Tiger*. I was expecting to be reassured by the sight of that red-headed woman lying on the bed. I'd rehearsed my opening line. 'This is Claudia,' I was going to say, waving a hand at the screen. But the image was of a different edition of the book – there was no woman and no bed, only a drawing of palm trees. Panic! But then I felt a rush of adrenaline. *'Moon Tiger',* I said, gesturing above and behind me, 'is one of my favourite novels. The heroine is called Claudia, and when we meet her she is dying.'

I talked about how I loved that book in particular – the sheer scope of the history of the world seen through the eyes of a dying woman – and books in general, and how what I most enjoyed about my job was the way that books offered a bridge between me and someone I'd never met before, and how some of the most profound moments of my life had happened on the shop floor in conversation with a customer I had just met. I shared some funny stories about Harrods, and one about an angry woman in Oxford Street who had sworn at me when I'd told her there was no new novel called *Julian and George* but suggested she might be looking for *Arthur & George* by Julian Barnes. I said how much I loved writing recommends cards, finding the right words to persuade customers into buying a book I adored, and how I saw myself as the last post on the journey between the author's mind and the reader's hand. I finished with a quick book recommendation – *Room* by Emma Donoghue – and the audience applauded.

That afternoon I walked to the tube thinking that I had enjoyed myself, that it had been exciting, that I'd really liked talking to the publishers afterwards. I'd like more of that, I thought. I'd like there to be more of that sort of thing in my life. And then I went to pick up Matt from the childminder's, and the next day I went to work and returned to the life of a bookshop manager – rota, payroll, cashing up, returns – and forgot about it.

A couple of months later I was offered a secondment to head office. I was delighted, not least because the building was only a ten-minute walk from our flat and the childminder's. Everything got a little bit easier logistically, though I was still overwhelmed by how hard it was to juggle caring for a baby and going out to work. Often I'd be in a meeting and look down to see a trail of baby snot along the sleeve of my cardigan.

At head office, I was made merchandising trials coordinator. The idea was that we could sell more books if we displayed them differently, so we had to think up new ways of organizing the travel section or dictionaries, and then test out the new plan in a few shops to see if it worked. I had to use Excel spreadsheets and was awful at it. I went on a course but that hardly helped. I needed to understand something called a VLOOKUP but could never tell whether it had worked or not. Erwyn kept trying to show me, but no matter how often I saw it done, I couldn't grasp it. I had my first and only migraine and saw flashing lights. The optician said my eyes didn't work well together but also that it was probably the stress of it. I kept dreaming that I'd sent the wrong bits of plastic to the wrong shops and everyone was angry with me. I dreaded being the originator of head office edicts that made no sense.

Thankfully, before I made some terrible error, I became the publisher relationship manager. This was right up my street: a wonderful role that involved lots of talking to people about books, and organizing things like competitions and author visits in order to get booksellers to rally behind specific titles. It was a privilege to set up activities for *The Night Circus* by Erin Morgenstern, *My Dear I Wanted to Tell You* by Louisa Young and *The Unlikely Pilgrimage of Harold Fry* by Rachel Joyce. At first I was very nervous around publishers – they seemed so shiny and glamorous and clever – but I soon got used to it, and to kissing people when I met them, though after a while I twigged that most people did an air kiss rather than the full-on smacker I was going for.

One of the books I worked on was *How To Be a Woman* by Caitlin Moran, whose feminism was exhilarating and funny. I started speaking up more and even asked for a pay rise. For ages I'd half fancied trying to write a blog about books but hadn't felt confident enough. Now I dived in. I wrote about *How To Be a Woman* and then shared it on Twitter. People liked it!

Then life took another turn. The *Evening Standard* was doing a literacy campaign called Get London

Reading and Waterstones wanted to make a contribution. I'd told someone about my dad and how he had struggled to read and write, so the *Standard* came and interviewed me about it at Piccadilly. Dad was so proud, and loved that his experience might be useful to other people. His pride jumped up another level when I was approached to work for Quick Reads, a charity that publishes short books for emergent adult readers. If I'd seen an advert, I wouldn't have had the gumption to apply, but lots of people encouraged me. My heart beat so hard through the interview that I thought surely everyone could hear it, but I settled in, answered the questions, was honest about what I didn't know, and talked a lot about my dad and what I'd learnt from him, including the Jane Eyre fiasco, and how his life had been hugely enriched by being able to think of himself as a reader. I talked about how I longed to break down the barriers that made people feel that books were not for them. That works of literature did not necessarily have to be difficult to read and that, if appointed, I would try to get a Booker Prize-winning author to write a Quick Read. 'That will be a tall order,' said my interviewer, but she was smiling. When she rang to offer me the job, I didn't need any thinking time and gave an immediate yes. My bookselling years were over.

Books about Reading

It can be easy to take our ability to read and our access to education for granted. These books explore situations where people either can't read or are prevented from learning, and explore the impact that has on the rest of their lives.

The Reader by Bernhard Schlink
When Michael is fifteen he has a brief love affair with an older women, Hanna, who likes him to read aloud to her. Years later, now a law student, Michael attends a trial of concentration camp guards and Hanna is in the dock. Why won't she defend herself and why is she agreeing to things that aren't true? It's a good title, *The Reader*. We think it refers to Michael, but it could also be about Hanna as she learns to read, and perhaps it is also about us as we turn the pages and consider our own ability to extend forgiveness to people who have done terrible things.

A Judgement in Stone by Ruth Rendell
'Eunice Parchman killed the Coverdale family because she could not read or write.' The first line of this mystery

reveals the 'who', and the rest explores why a cleaner takes revenge on her employers in such a brutal way and how she is ultimately caught out by her failure to destroy written evidence.

Rivals by Jilly Cooper

Taggie O'Hara is the daughter of a famous journalist and a celebrated actress. Her brother and sister are highly intelligent and she feels like the odd one out because she is dyslexic, doesn't know her left from her right, and has no skills apart from cooking. It comes good for Taggie in the end, as Rupert Campbell-Black falls for her sweet nature. This book was written when we were much less aware of dyslexia, and I've lost count of the number of people who have told me it helped them to recognize what the struggles of friends and family were about.

Instructions for a Heatwave by Maggie O'Farrell

Gretta is baking bread when her husband pops out for a newspaper and doesn't come back. It's the long, hot summer of 1976 and Robert's disappearance brings his troubled grown-up children back to the family home. Aoife, the youngest, arrives from New York, where her job as an assistant to a photographer has gone wrong because she daren't admit she can't read.

I Am Malala by Malala Yousafzai

In October 2012, Taliban gunmen boarded a school bus, looking for the girl who had become known as an advocate for education. 'Who is Malala?' they asked. 'I am Malala,' said Malala, and they shot her in the face. This is a story of the everyday and the miraculous, of the bravery of one young girl growing up in a society where the rights of women to education are not accepted.

On Earth We're Briefly Gorgeous by Ocean Vuong

'I am writing to reach you – even if each word I put down is one word further from where you are.' A boy called Little Dog writes a letter to his mother who can't read. There has always been love between them, but also violence that erupts without warning when she is tired from working at the nail parlour and breathing in the fumes all day. If she could understand his words, would he be free to tell this story of their journey from Vietnam to America?

From Reader to Writer

I started my new job at Quick Reads on 23 April 2012, which was Shakespeare's birthday and World Book Night. There was so much to learn! I had to commission the books and also make sure they were being used as widely as possible. I was familiar with my dad's story, but I quickly found out that there were many and varied reasons why people might have arrived in adulthood without the ability to read and write well. Our books were on offer in bookshops and libraries and used in adult learning settings, in literacy classes for refugees who had recently arrived in the country, and in prison.

My first prison visit was to Pentonville, a large, forbidding building in North London that had been completed in the 1840s. As I went through the security checks, emptying my bags and pockets to show that I wasn't trying to smuggle anything in, my hands started to tremble and I thought how much worse it must feel to be visiting a loved one, rather than going in to talk about books. On this visit I was with Andy McNab, who had just written a Quick Read for us about his journey into reading. Andy had been abandoned as a baby, and had been recruited into the army from Borstal. The army had taught him to read. We were at Pentonville so that Andy could give out certificates to those prisoners who had completed the Six Book Challenge, a scheme run by The Reading Agency that encouraged new readers to commit to completing six books.

We went into a big room full of men in grey joggers and Andy stood at the front. He told them how the army educator had changed his life by saying to him, 'You're not thick. You're just uneducated.' Then he handed out the certificates. I had been a little sceptical when I'd heard about the challenge, but was moved by how much it clearly meant to every single person who was applauded as he walked up to shake Andy's hand.

'It's amazing,' I whispered to the prison librarian sitting next to me.

'Most of them will never have been clapped for before,' she said. 'This is the first time they are getting a public well done.' That blew my mind. I thought of my school certificates for achievement, those appearances in plays, and what it would feel like never to have experienced any of it. The hairs on the back of my neck stood on end and I had a real sense that I was in the right place and had found a way to do meaningful work.

I was shocked and ashamed that I hadn't given much thought to prison before, and that I hadn't known of the low levels of literacy and high proportion of care leavers amongst inmates. As I met and talked with more people, I increasingly saw how many of them had been failed by society again and again. I'd get into arguments with friends who wanted to see criminals punished. 'You'd give money to the NSPCC, wouldn't you?' I'd say. 'Prison is full of adults who never got any support or guidance when they were younger. It has to be about rehabilitation.'

I loved the prison work. It was hard and harrowing and I'd cry on the way home, but I felt very moved when I could see that I had managed to shift the way people thought about reading. As I kept explaining to nice, well-meaning publishing and charity types, if someone can't read as an adult, they will usually have had a bad experience of education. Often they will not see reading as a source of comfort and joy, but rather as an instrument of humiliation and worry, like the man I met who had grown up in care. He'd been in a dormitory with five other boys and only two of them were still alive. He said that when you are struggling to survive, education slips down the list of priorities.

I started telling the people I met in prison about my dad because it helped them to trust me. Dad hadn't ever been to prison but he'd had the occasional night in the cells, sometimes for being drunk, sometimes for being Irish in the wrong place and at the wrong time. I'd talk about his childhood, which resonated hugely with my audience, many of whom had been bereaved as children and had known poverty. One day a man said, 'Thanks for telling us about your dad. It's amazing to me that someone who sounds a bit like me could have a daughter who turns into someone like you.'

Much as I thought reading was enriching, I didn't think people who couldn't read were failures. I loved my dad before he could read and would love him just as much if he'd never learnt. This was a bit of an eye-opener for people, and not the usual thing that a literacy charity person would say. I wanted people to read because I hoped it would be a great thing for them, not because I needed to convert everyone into good citizens. I didn't want people to read in the same way they might eat five portions of fruit and vegetables every day, but because I wanted them to know the mind-expanding privilege of walking a mile in someone else's shoes, of being able to turn a page and be transported to another world.

This would cause conflict with our funders. To get money, we had to prove that our books would help people to read, and thus make them more productive and less likely to be a drain on society and commit crime.

I thought this was true, but also knew it wasn't the way to encourage any battered, scarred individual into confronting their fears and giving it a go. I also fought a battle over evaluation – if I was taking part in a prison reading group, I knew it was a bad idea to try to make people fill in a form. Probably around half of them wouldn't be able to read or write well enough and wouldn't want to have to admit it in front of the others, and even those who were capable of completing the form would feel suspicious about its purpose.

Were it not for my dad, I could see that my ease with books and my unchecked evangelical fervour for reading might have led me to inadvertently put people off. I had to love reading to be an advocate for it, but empathy was more important because I needed to understand people's fear.

Although I'd always found reading easy, driving had not come so naturally. It had been the most difficult thing I'd ever learnt to do, and I could do it, but only just, and certainly not when under pressure. One day, when attempting to parallel park outside my flat, I kept getting it wrong and hitting the kerb. I began to panic and felt a heave in my tummy and an unpleasant prickling under my arms. I tried to take a deep breath but then there was a car behind me so I had to hurry up. I just about managed it, and got out of the car to a round of applause from a group of builders up on some scaffolding on the flats next door. I gave them a rueful wave, while feeling I might throw up into the gutter, and then walked home on wobbly legs and had a good cry on the sofa. I realized that the feeling I had when my back wheels hit the kerb for the fourth time was how someone would feel in a prison reading group if they had to take a turn reading aloud. So, I started telling people about my driving and that always broke the ice nicely. And I resolved not to get anyone to read aloud but to focus instead on talking about the story and the themes.

There was magic in this. It meant people could appreciate the books irrespective of their skill levels. Those who would feel reluctant if they were asked to talk about themselves directly would soon be telling personal anecdotes inspired by what had happened in the book. Often these hints and fragments of stories would be extremely sad, and I could see what a terrible thing it was to be stuck in a story over which you had no control and little understanding.

It was astonishing for people to start to think that they could be the sort of person who read books. We got a letter from someone who had started off with a Quick Read and was now on Dante, and my favourite ever comment was, 'Now I read books like I was born to it,' which made me ponder what we get as a birthright and how much that depends on our circumstances.

Quick Reads was a part-time role, so I was casting about for something else to do. I'd been keeping up my blog as, much as I loved my new job, I missed reading new books and talking to strangers about them. Often, when walking through a bookshop – I arranged to have most of my meetings in bookshop cafes – I would see customers mulling over the back cover of something I loved and be unable to resist striking up a conversation. This was the meat and drink of bookselling life, but less easy to do while wearing my coat and clearly not working there.

I started up a book club on Twitter and we decided to meet in real life. We read *Heartburn* by Nora Ephron and, rather by coincidence, we met in the Old Crown on New Oxford Street, where a few years earlier I'd had a humiliating episode with the man whose voice I wouldn't want to hear if I was dying. It was great fun to talk about Ephron turning her heartbreak into a book and I wasn't the only one to share a personal story. One woman told us that a friend of hers had, like Ephron, been seven months pregnant when she found out about her husband's affair, with the twist being that the husband's lover was also seven months pregnant. The surprisingly happy ending was that the man was long gone, but the women and the children they bore at the same time were great friends.

Later that year, I was offered a job at the *Bookseller* as maternity leave cover for the Books Editor. I had to write a long article about the fiction coming out each month, and choose which titles to highlight. Because the column came out four months before publication, I'd have to read a manuscript because even the proofs wouldn't be ready. I was halfway through Julian Barnes's *The Sense of an Ending* at home one day, when I left the room for a few minutes and came back to find that Matt had spread the manuscript pages over the floor and was happily crayoning all over them. Matt's first three-word sentence was 'Mummy read book,' an observation rather than a request, as I was lying on the sofa absorbed in *The Marriage Plot* by Jeffrey Eugenides. (I do always worry this sounds a bit smug, so in the interest of balance, dear reader, let me tell you that his first four-word sentence was, 'Big poo in there.')

I would try to read the start of as many novels as possible – often thirty or forty – and then would finish at least fifteen new books every month. 'How do you do it?' people asked, and the honest answer was that I didn't like TV and had no other hobbies. Sometimes I would go pleasantly crazy. After finishing *Life After Life* by Kate Atkinson, in which Ursula Todd keeps dying and then having another chance at life, I felt spaced out but had to go grocery shopping. The young man at the checkout asked me how I was. 'I feel a bit peculiar, actually,' I said. 'I've been reading too many books and the one I've just finished invites you to think of the untravelled roads, the paths not taken, so I've been considering my own life and all the different ways everything might have worked out. It's quite disorientating, isn't it? I feel quite strange.'

He looked at me for a moment and then said, 'Do you want a bag?' which was the perfect response, really. I told Erwyn about it and then he too would quite often listen as I went off on a flight of fancy, pause, and then say, 'Do you want a bag?'

When I picked *A Little Life* by Hanya Yanagihara off my teetering pile of proofs at the *Bookseller* office, I only intended to read a couple of chapters, but was so enthralled by Jude and whether or not he would be able to find a way to live with his suffering that I stayed up all night, still turning the pages, and felt extremely odd the next day as I went about my business feeling like I was hovering between this world and Yanagihara's fictional one.

My days were full of meaning and purpose and books and authors and, remembering how I used to get told off for bringing the *Bookseller* back from my break smelling of fags, I felt my dreams had come true. It had taken longer than it would do in a book, but the transformation I longed for when I worked at Harrods had happened. I felt really good, and (other than a little confusion over what was real and what I'd read about in a book) saner and happier than ever before. I knew that it suited me to be busy and to have a reason to read.

My two jobs meant I would often have vastly different experiences in the same day, like when I spent the morning with a reading group in Pentonville and the evening at the British Library for the launch of a new literary prize. I loved everything that involved readers and writers but found the fundraising terrifying. Much of the success of Quick Reads depended on publishers being willing to fund the costs of their writers being involved, so I'd go to meetings in publishers' boardrooms seeking their support, and would ask them to use their imaginations to travel with me far away from this beautiful room in Central London to a prison where half the inmates could barely read.

The first time I went to Downing Street, Dad was very chuffed. He kept asking me questions about how I'd get in and I saw that he just couldn't believe his daughter was going to Downing Street. He continued to inspire me as I found myself in more and more social situations that were both exciting and intimidating. He told me how when he went to London in his late teens with his shipmates, they went to a restaurant where they had printed menus. He was flummoxed but sat tight, let his friends order, and then said, 'I'll have what he's having.' I thought of this a lot whenever I was unsure of anything. All I had to do was hold steady and watch what everyone else did. In time, I learnt that it doesn't really matter, and that no one who is worth anything cares if you use the wrong knife. The important thing was not to be rendered less effective because I was overawed by my surroundings.

When our 2014 list was due to come out, we featured my dad and his story in our PR campaign. We held a launch party at Waterstones Piccadilly where I introduced Dad to lots of publishers. One of them said to me afterwards, 'You never told us how handsome he is,' which made Dad laugh a lot. After the party we went up to Manchester by train to go on *BBC Breakfast* the next morning. As we waited in the green room, a researcher came in and asked us to sign the legal release forms. I saw Dad go pale as he looked at the two pages of densely typed words. Like the *Jane Eyre* introduction, he didn't know he wasn't supposed to read every word and it felt too much for him, in a situation where he was focused on the fact that he'd have to tell his story on telly in a few minutes' time. I smiled at him, gave the form a quick scan, and pointed out to him where to sign. No one else in the room noticed this moment of panic, and I thought again how much my dad's experiences had helped me with my job. He was brilliant in the studio and then we went on Radio 4 together. Mum said, 'Dad sounds really Irish and you sound really posh.'

The following year, I organized a partnership with the Booker Prize. Roddy Doyle – who had won in 1993 for *Paddy Clarke Ha Ha Ha* – wrote us a brilliant Quick Read called *Dead Man Talking* and the prize funded reading groups in prison with it. On publication day we went to Brixton Prison in the morning and then had a launch event at the House of Commons, and I told our guests that we were giving them the same book that we'd handed out in Brixton that morning, to enable a rare shared cultural experience. I also joked that reading books had taught me how to behave in fine places, and that it was thanks to *The Bell Jar* by Sylvia Plath that I'd never drunk the contents of a finger bowl, because Esther Greenwood had done exactly that the first time she encountered one.

Books were helpful to me in this odd new life as novels are full of characters who feel like outsiders. Like my beloved Anne Shirley, I was often nervous and my imposter syndrome raged, though it helped to find out there was a name for it and that it wasn't only me who expected to be found out and evicted. Still, I continually worried I'd expose myself in some way. The first time I went to a meeting at the House of Lords I was so stunned by the sense of history, the scale of the pageantry, I could hardly speak. I got used to it, though. Familiarity made it just another place.

One day, I was coming out of the toilets when an elderly lady attracted my attention. 'My dear,' she said conspiratorially, and gestured behind me. I realized that my skirt was tucked up in my tights. As I sorted myself out I felt a strange relief. Now that I'd showed my pants off in the House of Lords and nothing terrible had happened, maybe I could try to worry less about everything. I was interviewing authors at festivals now and getting used to the rather intimidating green rooms. I began to feel at home, and supremely grateful that I was paid to read books and encourage others to do so, too.

And then I started to write again. Something about being up close to the makers of books helped me to see that the only thing stopping me from writing one myself was my own reluctance. I had been investing the process with too much mystery and reverence, and as the Quick Reads that had started out as conversations between me and the author turned into manuscripts and then into books, I could see it really was a case of putting one word in front of another. So many times I'd tried to write about what happened to Matty and so many times it had proved too hard. Could I have another go?

This time I didn't give up. I knew by now that there was no way of escaping the story, that if I stopped writing it I'd just be back again in a few months' time, still trapped, still unable to write anything else. And meanwhile my son Matt was learning to speak and asking questions about the world. I had a tiny photo of Matty and me in my purse and one day, as I was paying at the supermarket, Matt leaned over and asked who it was. I was filled with a sense of panic. I knew I mustn't tell him lies. I'd long observed – in fiction and in life – that secrets in families were always bad news.

I tapped away, early in the morning and late into the night. On Sundays we'd go to Kew Gardens, and Erwyn and Matt would leave me in the Orangery for two hours while they went to feed the birds. I didn't think anyone would ever want to read what I was writing, but it was important to me to keep going.

Spending time with people in prison taught me that it is a terrible thing to carry around a story you don't fully understand. I'd been so used to thinking I couldn't write because I was too stupid or common, or not clever enough, or not posh enough, but my prison work helped me see that, comparatively, I was phenomenally skilled and fortunate. If I was asking people in prison to get over what had happened to them – often dreadful, soul-destroying things – then surely I had to listen to my own advice.

Memoirs

I was never a huge reader of memoir compared to fiction until I tried to write one, and then I found an appreciation for the form that continues to grow as I learn more about the craft and art of writing about the self. Most of my favourite memoirs don't only tell the author's story, but also include reflections on the nature of memory, truth and narrative in a way that I find endlessly fascinating.

I Know Why the Caged Bird Sings by Maya Angelou
'I hadn't so much forgot as I couldn't bring myself to remember.' The first of seven volumes of autobiography, *I Know Why the Caged Bird Sings* takes us to Stamps, Arkansas in the 1930s where Maya and her brother Bailey are being brought up by their grandmother. Maya has to navigate racism and rape, yet somehow remains full of hope, and this book – and all her writing – has so much wisdom to offer: 'She comprehended the perversity of life, that in the struggle lies the joy.'

Why Be Happy When You Could Be Normal? by
Jeanette Winterson

'When my mother was angry with me, which was often, she said, "The Devil led us to the wrong crib."' I am fascinated when authors explore the same material in both fiction and non-fiction, and this memoir of adoption, mothering and madness revisits territory that will be familiar to readers of *Oranges Are Not the Only Fruit*. It is both an excoriating and illuminating personal story and a meditation on writing and truth: 'Truth for anyone is a very complex thing. For a writer, what you leave out says as much as those things you include.'

All at Sea by Decca Aitkenhead

The author's partner Tony, a drug dealer with a complex past and a huge heart, used to joke to her that an internet dating site would never have matched them up. This is the sad but beautiful story of their unlikely love affair, the family they created, and how everything changed when one of their sons was caught by the tide and Tony had to swim out to save him but never made it safely back to shore.

When Breath Becomes Air by Paul Kalanithi

Neurosurgeon Paul Kalanithi had always wanted to write, and so that's what he did when he was diagnosed with inoperable lung cancer and knew he only had a few months of life left. The result is beautiful and strangely invigorating. 'The word "hope" first appeared in English about a thousand years ago, denoting some combination of confidence and desire. But what I desired – life – was not what I felt confident about – death.'

The Return by Hisham Matar

'At times a whole year will pass by without seeing the sun or being let out of this cell.' In 1990 the author's father was kidnapped in Cairo by the Egyptian secret police, delivered to Qaddafi and imprisoned in Abu Salim in Tripoli. In this memoir, Matar writes of exile and home, of his attempts to discover the fate of his father, and of how he has lived with grief laced with uncertainty.

Clothes, Clothes, Clothes. Music, Music, Music. Boys, Boys, Boys. by Viv Albertine

'Anyone who writes an autobiography is either a twat or broke. I'm a bit of both.' Viv Albertine became the guitarist in the all-female punk band the Slits in an era when the role of women was to be the girlfriends of the band, not the band itself. This memoir of sex, drugs and punk tells the full story, with joy and squalor jostling for the upper hand. It is full of gems: Viv starts the look of wearing Dr Martens with skirts because she needs to be able to run away when Sid Vicious gets her into trouble. Her next memoir, *To Throw Away Unopened*, is also brilliant.

Cheerful Charlie

It still feels magical to me that the tapping and scribbling ended up being published as a memoir, *The Last Act of Love.* I had started out imagining that no one would read it, but as I showed bits to a couple of supportive friends, I did begin to believe that the pages could be a book one day. And then I got a brilliant and kind agent who worked with me to find a brilliant and kind editor, and I continued to put one word in front of another. I know that I couldn't have started the book if I'd thought about it being read, but wouldn't have had the stamina to finish it without the prospect of a reader. It was hard work in every way, but also exciting, and I loved seeing the stages on the journey from author to reader from the other side. I found the cover design process fascinating, and printed out the possible options and stuck them up on my wall. Matt's little friends would ask what they were when they came around to play.

'Mummy is writing a book about her brother who died,' Matt would say, and I'd think what a tremendous way we had come from having one tiny photo hidden away in my purse.

It is an amazing thing to go from being the hand-maiden of other people's books to having one of your own out in the world, and I had to pinch myself when I saw it in the windows of my favourite shops. I loved the displays, which often involved chalkboard art of dart-boards or little pictures of me and Matty. I had a launch party at Waterstones Piccadilly and sat at the half-moon table in Hatchards to sign stock. I went on *BBC Breakfast* and back to Snaith, where I was interviewed in the pub.

Many wonderful things happened but it was more complex than I would have imagined. So few people in my current life had known about Matty or that I was writing. One said, 'I can't believe we've been friends for ten years and I never knew anything about this.' In some ways I felt like I had blown my cover. I'd abandoned my carefully constructed amiable bookworm disguise and told my secrets in one go.

I shouldn't have been so shocked to find out it could be tricky. I had read about it in a collection of essays about writerly shame called *Mortification*, in which drunken poets and fragile novelists end up in humiliating situations all over the world. The essays are very funny. My favourites include Don Paterson's night out in the best curry house in Goole, and Simon Armitage's stream of anecdotes that culminates in him finding a copy of his own book in a charity shop. He opens it and sees his handwriting on the dedication page: 'To Mum and Dad.'

Deborah Moggach is good on the idea that writers can only really moan about this to each other; who else cares if 'we sit alone and unloved beside our pile of books, approached only once in two hours and that by a woman who is trying to flog us her self-published book on recovering from breast cancer? Or that we wait, alone in the darkness, on the deserted platform at Newark station, the only reading matter a VIOLENT ASSAULT: WITNESSES WANTED sign swinging in the wind, until we realize we've missed the last train home.'

When I first read *Mortification* I thought it was funny, but I didn't really think it was true. I was sure these writers would be protected from shame by the massive metaphorical comfort blanket of being actual published writers. I expected that the very state of 'being a writer' would create an undimmable glow. But I was wrong, and it took me a long time to stop chastising myself for being ungrateful and to settle back down into normal life.

Being a writer brings all sorts of wonderment – I adore letters from readers; I adore having readers – but it is not as satisfying or comfortable as I imagined, and I now have a long list of my own mortifications. Sometimes it doesn't help to know the secrets of backstage. Arriving at a London Waterstones one evening to interview another author, I presented myself at the front desk. 'Who?' asked the bookseller when I said my name, despite the fact that he was literally – because my face was on the cover of my book – de-stickering me. It was the oddest feeling to know that those books were about to go into returns crates and that my time on a table was over.

The trick is to feel entitled to nothing and to treat everything good that happens as a delightful surprise, but this can be easier said than done. Luckily, I like talking to strangers so much that the plentiful mortifications of the book tour are balanced out with stimulating conversations on and off stage.

'Isn't it strange,' someone once said to me, 'that people who have read your book think they know you?'

'They do know me,' I said. 'Anyone who has read *The Last Act of Love* knows me far better than someone who knows me in real life but hasn't.' I'm far more truthful in writing than in person, though one of the great pleasures of book events is that we know what we are there for, that we can mainline straight into discussing love and death, and don't have to do the dance of everyday life where we pretend to be normal so that we don't frighten the horses. I enjoy the way my book catapults me into intimate conversation with anyone who has read it.

The attention went to my head a bit. After so many years of feeling like a nobody on the shop floor, I was surprised that people were nice to me and seemed to care about my opinions. I felt a bit like Anne Shirley when Mrs Barry gets out the best china for her and offers different types of cake, as though she is proper company.

As I settled into my new life, I escaped into other people's books in exactly the same way I did when I started working at Harrods. Then, I'd found comfort and solace on the shop floor. Now I love mentoring and teaching and interviewing writers at festivals and reviewing books. I like getting further back in the journey from the author's mind to the reader's hand, and my own struggles with writing are transformed into something useful when I can help my students to wrestle their experiences onto the page. My prison work is deeper now that I do writing workshops and try to figure out meaningful exercises for a group where many of the participants can't write in sentences, but have so many stories that want to burst out of them.

The only problem I have with reviewing is that I never want to say anything bad about a book. In the same way that having a baby tenderized me to the fate of babies, having a book out makes me feel protective of all books. I am capable of seeing that a baby is ugly or a book is badly put together, but it still seems like a miracle that it exists at all, and I certainly don't want to be the person who points out any flaws to the poor parent.

Recently I went to Belfast to do an event and was chatting with the taxi driver who picked me up from the airport.

'What's your first book about?'

'It's about the death of my brother.'

'What's your other book about?'

'It's about grief and loss more generally.'

'Well, you're a Cheerful Charlie, aren't you?'

I rocked with laughter.

On my flight home I finished rereading *The Year of Reading Dangerously* by Andy Miller. I laughed so hard that I disturbed the man sitting next to me.

'Must be good,' he said.

'It is!' I said, and started to tell him about it.

'I don't read books,' he said. 'I haven't got time.' And he went back to looking at Excel spreadsheets and graphs on his computer.

So much of human interaction – whether as a barmaid, a bookseller or a writer – is working out who wants to talk and who doesn't, and being happy with whatever is on offer. I felt lucky that I don't have to grapple with Excel any more, but could spend time going out into the world meeting interesting strangers and seeing old friends. I felt glad to be on my way home with a book that was making me think and laugh. I felt like a Cheerful Charlie, as I often do.

A few days later, I was on a train and fell into conversation with the three women sharing my table. They lived in Falmouth and were on their way to New York to celebrate a 'significant' birthday. They looked older than sixty but younger than seventy, I thought, and two of them were sisters. We talked about life in Falmouth. They were still using the wooden surfboards they'd had since childhood, and explained how they feel different to modern ones and how they often lend them to young surfers who are amazed at the experience. I told them I had never seen a wooden surfboard in real life, but that Agatha Christie was an early advocate and there are photos of her on the beach with her board.

This led to talk of reading and writing. We talked about New York, about martinis and Manhattans, and *By Grand Central Station I Sat Down and Wept* by Elizabeth Smart and *What I Loved* by Siri Hustvedt. We got onto Georgette Heyer and they agreed that it was better to describe her as a historical P. G. Wodehouse rather than Regency Mills & Boon. 'You *do* know a lot about her,' said one of the ladies as we compared notes on Heyer's best books. They asked about whether I liked spending time with other writers and I said I did, because it was always good to hear someone else talk about their doubts and insecurities and helped me to remember that it's all part of the process. 'Georgette Heyer was very scathing about other writers,' I said. 'She called them inkies and thought they spent too much time complaining.'

I loved books about books long before I got my job in a bookshop, but these days I have a vested interest in portrayals of writers and their friendships. In *The Silkworm* by Robert Galbraith, an author who is suspected of murder tells Cormoran Strike that writers are a savage breed: 'If you want life-long friendship and selfless camaraderie, join the army and learn to kill. If you want a lifetime of temporary alliances with peers who will glory in your every failure, write novels.'

Books about Writers

I'm fascinated by how life makes the journey onto the page. Some writers are aggravated by questions about whether or not their work is autobiographical, but I think that most fiction is – not in a literal sense but because everyone writes to their preoccupations and wounds. Not all writers want to admit to that, and why should they? As Hilary Mantel's Thomas Cromwell says: 'It is wise to conceal the past even if there is nothing to conceal. A man's power is in the half-light, in the half-seen movements of his hand and the unguessed-at expression of his face. It is the absence of facts that frightens people: the gap you open, into which they pour their fears, fantasies, desires.'

I Capture the Castle by Dodie Smith
'I write this sitting in the kitchen sink.' There are two writers in this delightful tale of an eccentric family living in a broken-down castle. I used to identify with Cassandra, who starts keeping a diary when she is seventeen and captures the interesting details about the rich

Americans who come to live next door, but now I fear I am more like her eccentric father, who has writer's block and doesn't want to do anything except be left alone to read detective novels.

The Blind Assassin by Margaret Atwood
'Ten days after the war ended, my sister Laura drove a car off a bridge.' One of my absolute favourite fictional devices is when we are not sure what we are reading or who has written it. There are multiple books within this book – an acclaimed novel, some pulp fiction, a photograph album, some exercise books – and they combine to tell a story of two sisters and their tangled relationships with two very different men.

The Silkworm by Robert Galbraith
When Cormoran Strike is visited by Leonora Quine, he agrees to find her missing husband and make him come home. Owen Quine is an author and often goes away for a while, but when Strike finds him he has been murdered in exactly the same horrible way as one of the characters in his yet to be published novel, *Bombyx Mori*. This is loads of fun and very good on author vanity. Quine equates the way silkworms must be boiled to produce silk with the way writers must suffer for their work.

The Infatuations by Javier Marías
On the way to her job in publishing, María has breakfast at the same cafe each day where she is always cheered by the presence of a couple who are deeply in love. When the man is brutally murdered and María offers condolences to his widow, she is drawn into an uneasy friendship. This is an absorbing literary murder mystery, but the best bits for me are María's many scathingly amusing frontline anecdotes about the vanity of authors and her colleagues in publishing.

Commonwealth by Ann Patchett
On the day of Franny Keating's christening, her mother kisses a neighbour and starts an affair that ends two marriages and creates a new family with six siblings. Twenty-six years later, Franny is working as a cocktail waitress in Chicago when she meets a famous author and tells him their secrets, never dreaming that he will put the story into a novel – it is called *Commonwealth* – or how her siblings will feel when they see themselves on the page.

Intimacy by Hanif Kureishi
Jay likes to write 'with a soft pencil and a hard dick – not the other way around.' We join him for the twenty-four-hour period where he decides whether or not to leave

his partner and their children. There's a very funny masturbation scene and a hilarious trip to a couples therapist who tries to make Jay read a bad poem aloud. I also enjoy the two-page diversion into Jay's stationery habits; he has at least fifty notebooks, all of which are blank apart from the first page. As a person, I disapprove of Jay and his inability to put the welfare of his children before his questing cock, but as a reader I find his selfishness exhilarating. As a writer, if this is an autobiographical novel, I'm envious of such aggressive and unapologetic mining of the self.

Back to Cornwall

In the summer of 2017, Erwyn, Matt and I moved from London down to Cornwall. I wanted to be near my parents after my dad had a bout of pneumonia that frightened us all. Sooner or later, I thought, something will happen, and I won't want to be on the sleeper train every few days, or bombing up and down the M5. I'd had no choice when Mum had cancer, but now that I could do most of my work from a computer and Erwyn had his own business selling stamps, there was no real need to stay in London.

Without knowing it, the house we bought in Falmouth was next door to the one in which my mother was born. Granny's family had moved there in 1943 so her father could manage the Lipton store on the high street. She met my grandad at the Odeon where he was a projectionist, and they had three children while continuing to live in her parents' house. My Aunt Marion gave me a photo of them on their wedding day, Easter Saturday 1950. They are standing in the garden and our house is in the background. It sits on my mantelpiece, and I often look at it just before I set off to go down to the library or to pick something up from the Falmouth Bookseller. I like that I am walking in their footsteps.

Once we had moved into the new house, I unpacked boxes of books and my dad and Uncle Paul built new shelves. Dad whistled and sang as he worked, and I thought how lucky I was to have been able to gather my family together. I arranged and rearranged my books on the shelves. As I started rereading them and writing about them I began to spot patterns between the books and my life.

Sometimes I had a vivid memory of when I first encountered something. Other books seemed to have always been a part of me. My copy of Mary Wesley's *Not That Sort of Girl* is missing its cover and has 'the Bell and Crown' written on the title page. A big pink cloth-bound hardback of *The Bone Clocks* by David Mitchell reminded me of turning the last page and then immediately reading it again, and then having so many strange dreams that I remain confused about which plotlines are in the book and which I have built upon in my sleep. As I weighed *A Little Life* by Hanya Yanagihara in my hands, I remembered reading it in one sleepless night and how

I stumbled through the following day hardly able to function.

A proof of *Life After Life* by Kate Atkinson, in which Ursula Todd gets to relive her life again and again and make different decisions, made me think again of those moments in my own life when another path was not taken. Growing up, where I lived and who I knew depended on where my dad could get work. What would I be like if the tin mines hadn't closed down? Or if we'd stayed in Scotland? Or if Dad had taken the job he was offered on the Channel Tunnel instead of buying the pub? My big fault-line is Matty's accident, and I have spent too much of my life pining for a version where it didn't happen. Were it not for Sophie, I wouldn't have met John, and without him I'd never have moved to London or lived in New York. If I'd stayed in Snaith, I don't think I would have written books because I'd still be thinking of writers as godlike creatures somehow different from me. If I hadn't hung out with Erwyn that Easter, might I have gone to work in Paris or Cork?

Do I have a child in these parallel universes? A little girl, perhaps, or one who has a different ethnicity from my own. Maybe my children speak French or have Irish accents. Or there might be no child, no lover, no companion. Without Erwyn's steadying influence, I might not have flourished. Perhaps I have never finished writing a book and therefore still think that doing so would make me uncomplicatedly and unreservedly happy. You can go mad with this stuff. It's like staring into the Mirror of Erised.

Back in the here and now, Matt and I enjoyed *The Lion, the Witch and the Wardrobe*. When Peter finds out that Narnia is real and that he should not have doubted Lucy, he says, 'I apologise for not believing you. I'm sorry. Will you shake hands?' We agreed to incorporate a bit of this directness into our daily lives.

I worked through the blue hardback of Daphne du Maurier's Cornish novels. *Jamaica Inn* is dark and *Frenchman's Creek* is rather silly but I like it, not least because I remember rowing up the Helford on a family holiday looking for the creek, and because it explores how a woman can hold on to her freedom, or not, once she has children. *My Cousin Rachel* is an oddly powerful book and I can never work out where I think the truth lies. It is an extremely good portrait of a besotted young man – there are lovestruck young women galore in literature but enamoured young men are much harder to find.

I saved *Rebecca* until last. It was wonderful to read about the azaleas at Manderley as I looked at them at the garden centre. For the first time in my adult life I had a garden, and when the news got too much I turned off the world for a while and cultivated it, enjoying both the Cornish flora and the vocabulary: camellias, hydrangea, agapanthus, fuchsia. The friendly postman told us that the tree at the front was a magnolia and would be magnificent come the spring. As I struggled to walk up the Cornish hills but enjoyed looking at the sea, I thought of Rose Peel in *Not That Sort of Girl* who, as she thinks back over her life while walking, notes that when she was younger she would not have been rendered breathless by the climb, but then would also not have appreciated the view.

I bought a set of knives and was chopping radishes when the new, sharp blade whooshed through the radish and sliced hard into my thumb. Blood everywhere. I found some blister plasters which did a good job. A few hours later I heard a manly scream from the kitchen. Erwyn had done exactly the same thing.

'It's because we're not used to the sharpness,' I said as I patched him up. 'What a thrill, your thumb instead of an onion.'

He looked a bit confused, so I explained that Sylvia Plath had written a poem about cutting her finger while chopping onions. 'They'd just moved to Devon to avoid literary life,' I said. 'Maybe they'd bought new knives and weren't used to the sharpness. It didn't work out very well for them, the move. Ted Hughes kept going back to London to experience literary life with other women.'

This incident made me want to read *The Bell Jar* again and I downloaded the audiobook, read in gloriously limpid tones by Maggie Gyllenhaal. One day I was in the kitchen listening to it when my parents dropped round. I turned it off and Dad asked if he should read it. Would it bring him down? He likes a good cry over a book and finds that to be a release but doesn't want to read about depression, especially if it feels very real. I said that I didn't think *The Bell Jar* was a depressing book, apart from knowing that it is autobiographical, given what happened to the author.

'What happened to the author?' said Matt.

I hadn't thought he was listening, but he has an instinct for homing in on precisely the sort of details I'd rather washed over him.

It was one of those parental moments where I had to decide in a flash how honest to be.

'She killed herself.'

'How?'

'With the gas oven in her kitchen.'

'Why?'

'Well.' I took a deep breath. 'It's complex, as it always is when people kill themselves. She was depressed. It was very cold. It had been a long, snowy winter and she'd been alone with two small children after her husband had left her. And she probably didn't understand what was happening to her. People didn't always understand that winter is hard for people prone to depression. And her book had just come out. That can be destabilizing. She went down to show one of her neighbours a review of it a couple of days before she died.'

Matt nodded and I hoped that was going to be it. I didn't want to lie but I didn't want him to ask about her children.

'She was married to Ted Hughes,' said Mum. 'A poet.'

'He wrote a lot about nature,' I said, making a face because I don't much enjoy nature writing, unless there are plenty of people in it. 'Foxes.'

'I like foxes.'

'Maybe you'll like him, then. Actually, there's a poem about a fox that I like because it is also about writing.' I googled 'The Thought Fox' but Matt had lost interest and wandered off.

I hoped I had done the right thing. It's a continual worry. How to be honest without expecting him to carry too much of the weight of life on his slender shoulders.

As we settled into life in Falmouth, I tried to keep away from the news and off social media and read through my favourite books instead, finding solace and consolation among the well-worn pages. I read the Cazalet Chronicles again, thinking back to how, when I first read them at Hatchards, I gave most of my attention to the love affairs of the young women. Now, I saw how well Howard writes about children. When Ellen explains that they are late because Neville lost his sandshoes, Neville says, 'I only lost one of them,' which is exactly the sort of thing Matt would have said at that age. Matt, too, would like to keep a jellyfish as a pet and would be upset and cross when it died.

The Light Years is a perfect cocktail of the personal and the political. The novel ends hopefully in the late summer of 1938 with the characters who had prepared for the prospect of war feeling a bit foolish. The reader knows that this optimism is misplaced and that they will shortly be plunged into years of mayhem.

Sometimes, when I reread a book I have the feeling that I'm done with it, that our long and happy relationship has come to an end. I have not reached this point with the Cazalets. Every reread reveals more, and I'm sure there is still richness to come. A friend asks me how I have time for all this rereading and I boggle at the question. It is the thing that keeps me sane. A book a day will keep the doctor away, I hope.

Can a book save your life? Or is this just, as Andy Miller puts it, 'a sort of media-friendly shorthand for "a book I really like and would be prepared to talk about for money"?'

There are a few books that changed my life because they prompted me to take action. Julian Barnes sent me to France, though that wasn't only his fault. Françoise Sagan and Gustave Flaubert need to take a bit of responsibility, too. *How To Be a Woman* by Caitlin Moran inspired me to write the blog which led to me being paid for writing about books, something I would have considered impossible and unachievable until about five minutes before it actually happened. That book also helped me to find my voice with my memoir, as did *Maggie & Me* by Damian Barr and *The Boy with the Topknot* by Sathnam Sanghera. They made me believe it was possible for someone like me to write a book, not just read them. I was thoroughly put off social media by the double whammy of *So You've Been Publicly Shamed* by Jon Ronson and *You* by Caroline Kepnes. Joe's use of social media to stalk his victims made me hyper-aware of what I was giving away about myself online, and Jon Ronson's book made me unwilling to witness mob action on Twitter and terrified that my own public shaming was just around the corner.

I used to often make life decisions because they would move the narrative on, which is not the wisest way to behave, though there was that time *The Colour of Heaven* made me dump a bad boyfriend. I'm not alone in having my romantic life influenced by books. My friend was on a beach reading *The Pursuit of Love*, and when Fabrice says that for him love lasts five years, she realized her own relationship had lasted exactly five years and she had had enough of it. Another friend admits, on the condition of strict anonymity, that she might not have had an affair were it not that she wanted to find out if it felt like her favourite novels said it did.

Fiction is a strange beast, and sometimes it is not good for me that I behave too much as though I am a character in a novel subject to dramatic irony and poetic justice. Life is nerve-racking for those of us who have too much imagination. If in a novel a person forgets their keys and has to go back to the house, some terrible discovery almost certainly awaits. In real life it almost certainly doesn't, but I find it very anxiety-inducing because I can't help speculating on the possible plot developments that might happen. I can't go running at night or in the woods because I know what happens to women when they do that in novels. When Matt was little and I was apart from him, I felt deeply uncomfortable ever admitting that I found being a mother hard because it felt like I was tempting fate and asking – in narrative terms – for him to fall off the climbing frame or be abducted.

Another danger of fiction is that our expectations are set too high and we think that we deserve Mr Darcy, though even Mr Darcy won't be like Mr Darcy once he and Elizabeth Bennet have a couple of kids to look after.

Writers' diaries and letters can give a more honest picture than novels. L. M. Montgomery created dreamboat Gilbert Blythe, but her journals show how her life was continually made difficult because her husband didn't like her being praised and admired. Whenever I read or hear about the husbands of female writers, it makes me much more inclined to feel grateful for my own. Unlike L. M. Montgomery's husband, Erwyn is happy for much of our life to revolve around me and, unlike Ted Hughes, he doesn't go off to London to have affairs with other women. He would not leave me alone in the freezing cold with small children to look after. So while romantic fiction might give us unrealistic expectations, reading about the husbands of other writers can be a helpful corrective.

Reading has saved my life, again and again, and has held my hand through every difficult time. Now, if I start to fray around the edges I know I need to reverse out of watching the news, deactivate social media, curfew myself on technology and banish all devices from my bedroom. I need to get in the bath or go to bed with a book.

It is not always bad to avoid feelings of distress by burying ourselves in reading. If life takes a dark turn, if we are struck by the storm of grief, then there are worse things to do than read to get us through the long nights.

I no longer drink alcohol, but when I did, reading helped to cap my excesses because I didn't like it when I got so drunk that the words wouldn't stay still and I couldn't read myself to sleep. Reading is respite care for the mind. When I read, my breathing slows. I calm down. I become interested and curious. When I had EMDR therapy I realized that reading might be soothing simply because it is a bilateral activity. Our eyes move rhythmically across the page and back again. This may be why I find it so comforting and why it doesn't really matter what I read, as long as it makes me want to keep moving my eyes from left to right.

Above all, I find it consoling to be reminded that I am not alone, that everything I feel has been felt before, that everything I struggle with has been perplexing others since the dawn of time. My favourite books are universal. They illuminate my own life as well as showing me the lives of others and leave me changed, my worldview expanded. When I turn the last page I rejoin the real world knowing I am only a tiny speck in it, one small piece in a gigantic jigsaw. My concerns may feel modern and specific to me, but really they are as old as time itself. How do I love people when I know that the pain of their death might kill me? How do I live well in an unfair world? How do I care about my fellow humans but not end up choked by my own empathy? How do I balance my desire for excitement with my need for solitude? Reading is often seen as an introvert activity but I think it is essential for extroverts like me. It is a way of being alone but never lonely.

We are hardwired to seek out connection with other humans and to look for love, which makes us vulnerable to pain. The only way not to suffer is not to love, and that would be suffering in itself.

Helpful Non-Fiction

Fiction is both an ally and a friend but not necessarily a blueprint for behaviour. Non-fiction can be useful for navigating the ups and downs and I like it more as I age, or perhaps it is simply that there are better books due to an explosion in – for want of a better term – intelligent self-help. Here is a list of helpful books which I come back to again and again to aid me with life's challenges. Everything matters.

The Unexpected Joy of Being Sober by Catherine Gray
I read this about a year after I'd given up drinking and wish I'd had it before. Some passages resonate so deeply that I feel like the author must have stolen my diary. It's helpful, useful, kind and funny, and I would highly recommend it to anyone who is unhappy with how and why and how much they drink. I used to feel that sober life could only ever be a gloomy trudge, but there is a bright future out there, full indeed of unexpected joy.

How to Break Up with Your Phone by Catherine Price
I was a late adopter of technology and shocked to find
myself addicted to my phone, to the point where I was
ignoring my family and damaging my health. I was
already doing much of what the author suggests in this
enjoyable book, but it is good to see information organized so well and to have what I was groping towards
confirmed with wit and style. And the best thing about
putting technology in its proper place – servant not
master – is that it liberates you to read more books. I
usually turn my phone off at about 6 p.m., then give my
brain the treat of a well-crafted long-form narrative, and
am much better for it.

The Book You Wish Your Parents Had Read by
   Philippa Perry
When we treat the inconvenient emotions of children as
negatives to be corrected, we teach them that the way
they feel is wrong and unacceptable. If we can hold
steady and see sadness, anger and fear as an opportunity
to learn more about our child, then we will deepen our
bond and possibly increase their capacity for happiness,
as it is the repression of emotions that leads to problems
in the long run. Optimism is also highly important. Our
children need us to behave as though we are confident

that they will get the hang of things. And we mustn't ignore them for our phones! No matter what is happening in the world, our job now is not to be glued to the news cycle but to keep our children company as they grow into themselves.

Grief Works by Julia Samuel

Julia Samuel is a therapist who describes grief as the tug of war between the pain of loss and the instinct to survive. I have passed this book on to so many people who have written to me or who I have met at events who, like me, were bemused that their grief didn't behave in a linear way. We have to do our grief work, but we don't need to do it alone, and this is a beautiful and comforting book that never shirks the pain in life but offers both hope and practical advice.

The Choice by Edith Eger

How do you survive when you have seen the worst of humanity? Edith Eger danced before Nazi officer Josef Mengele at Auschwitz and was moments from death when she was pulled from a pile of bodies by a liberating soldier. Years later she became a therapist, and the stories of her clients are woven into this conversation about loss, grief, trauma and hope. She is generous, wise and extremely good company on the page. She believes there should be no hierarchy of human pain: 'I don't want you to hear my story and say, "My own suffering is less significant." I want you to hear my story and say, "If she can do it, then so can I!"'

With the End in Mind by Kathryn Mannix
Death will come and there is little to fear and much to prepare for. Mannix is a hospice doctor who writes about death not as an unjust and outrageous insult or inconvenient party pooper, but as the intended and inevitable final event of our lives. There are lessons to be learnt in how at the end of their lives people look back with a mixture of satisfaction and regret. What could we be doing now to redress the balance? Living with the end in mind seems to help me spend less time drowning in fear and worry, and more time looking up and appreciating the world. As Mannix says: 'There are only two days with fewer than twenty-four hours in each lifetime, sitting like bookends astride our lives: one is celebrated every year yet it is the other that makes us see living as precious.'

Books Revisited

Looking back, can I find myself? Can I connect to the little girl I once was, all those previous selves? I think so. I still prefer books to anything else and would rather have a book token than any other kind of present. I still ignore my friends and neglect my family to carry on reading, and it remains nearly impossible for me to stop reading something when I'm within grasping distance of the end. I have no idea how people can tolerate soap operas; it would torture me to be left on a cliffhanger and have to wait for the next episode three times a week.

I have been known to be less than truthful about what this distance is. Recently we had planned a family outing and when Erwyn shouted up the stairs to see if I was ready, I said, 'I'll just finish my book. I've only a few pages left.'

Matt bolted up the stairs to examine the evidence. 'That's much more than a few pages, Mummy. I've noticed you often tell lies about how much book you've got left so we'll let you finish it.'

'You are very perceptive and clever,' I said, 'and the sooner you let me get on with it, the sooner I'll be ready.'

Finding a new book I love remains one of my greatest pleasures in life. The last time I stayed up too late it was with *The Confessions of Frannie Langton* by Sara Collins. I felt the old familiar tingle in my fingers as I ran them over the embossed gold scissors on the front cover. I turned the last page at 3 a.m. and then lay in the dark, thinking how fiction has this great power to illuminate injustice and help us to see the world through another's eyes. Many of the best novels I've read in the last few years have been about slavery, like this one – *Homegoing* by Yaa Gyasi, *The Underground Railroad* by Colson Whitehead and *Washington Black* by Esi Edugyan – and their writers use the power of story to seek and uncover essential truths from the past which remain too relevant to the present.

Even as they shine a light on human cruelty, books teach us to give others the benefit of the doubt. I am inclined to believe people in life, because in books unlikely stories always turn out to be true and I never want anyone to feel like Lucy did when she came back from Narnia, or like Frannie does when she is judged and badly treated by people who can't conceive of what her life has been like. A little while ago I couldn't find my iPad, and the cynical part of me thought that Matt had done something with it or maybe broken it and been afraid to tell. He said he hadn't, so I took him at his word and it remained a mystery for days until I found it had slipped down behind my bedside table. I confessed to Matt that I'd doubted him: 'I'm sorry,' I said. 'I was wrong. Will you shake hands?'

Am I too naive? I've been told many times that I am. If I am, like Cassandra in *I Capture the Castle* it is a conscious naivety. I would rather be screwed over every so often than move through life expecting the worst. The pub gave me an effective radar; I am a good judge of character and not easily duped. The most important thing about life, as it was behind the bar and in every shop, is not to let an unpleasant vocal minority give you a distaste for the whole endeavour. I do still believe that most people have a better nature and it is worth putting effort into trying to unearth it. We need to find a way to be optimistic about the future. I know it is essential for me to keep faith in humanity, and that if too much exposure to real life – or life as it is sliced and diced by news channels – challenges my ability to do that, then I need to hide in books until I feel better.

I still always long to know what people are reading on trains and buses, will crane my head trying to see covers, and am alive to the possibility of starting up a conversation. One of the great delights of going to literary festivals is to be surrounded by other bookworms, to see them everywhere, in the cafes and the hotel dining rooms. These periods of talking to strangers about books make me truly happy.

And I still love to reread. I find an extraordinary joy in turning the pages of something I've encountered many times before. It is part of the great magic of books that they reveal more aspects to themselves as we grow into them.

It is a miracle to have a baby and for that baby to grow into a real-life boy. Perhaps the best rereading I do is with Matt. We've been reading and discussing Harry Potter for years. Recently, he and Erwyn went on a boys' trip to Holland and came home via Comic Con. As I picked them up from the train, I saw Matt was wearing a green hat.

'I'm a Slytherin,' he said shyly. 'I know you think I'm Gryffindor but I'm not.'

'You must be who you are, darling,' I said.

One of my challenges as a mother has been to cope with my fear that something bad will happen to Matt. Talking about Harry and his mum has always helped me to communicate my love to Matt: I will say that our hearts are joined by a golden thread that would outlast death. On his last birthday, his friend gave him a Harry Potter Lego set which showed the scene in *The Prisoner of Azkaban* where Harry charges down the Dementors by conjuring a Patronus in the shape of a stag. 'You can have this for your desk, Mum,' Matt said, giving me the model of the stag. Matt has not found reading easy but loves stories. I read to him; we do half an hour before school every morning and before bed every night and have just finished a – lightly censored by me – reading of Adrian Mole.

I no longer race through books. I have slowed down. During my bookselling days I always knew the order of every series and every author, but now my memory drifts and plays tricks. It deserted me during pregnancy and never quite came back, and now, when I ask my brain to give me bibliographic details, I feel as though I am opening the drawer of a filing cabinet to find it empty. I try not to mind too much, and flirt with the consoling theory that wisdom replaces memory as we age. I spent ten days rereading *Anna Karenina* and scribbling down my thoughts. When I then left my notebook on a train, it was a lowering realization that if I wanted to know what those thoughts were, I'd have to read the novel again. All I had in my brain was a feeling that I now have more in common with Levin than with Anna, and a rather weary surprise that Anna goes to so much bother for Vronsky.

Sadly I am still inclined to be hard on myself, to worry that I am not good enough, to compare myself to those around me and feel inadequate. Why must we do this, we sorry humans? Why is it so easy to get stuck in the mud of compare and despair? Sometimes I think I've spent my whole life worrying that I'm either too clever or not clever enough. I'm in situations where I think I'll be punished for using too many long words, or mocked because I might mispronounce something or expose the vast gaps in my knowledge. Even with reading it is too easy to get in a panic and decide that the fact I haven't read everything means I have no right to love books. I know this is wrong, and it breaks my heart when I see others do it, but I tumble into it myself. Don't do it, dear reader. Don't allow anything to dent your reading pleasure. Don't let anyone tell you that what you like isn't proper, that what brings comfort and ease to your soul isn't good enough.

I still feel like a bookseller by inclination and habit. I was recently in the glorious National Trust bookshop at Trelissick Garden, where the two ladies who worked there were puzzling over the order of the Hunger Games books.

'I can probably help,' I said, 'I've read them.'

I worked it out, and the lady told me she used to be a librarian and now enjoyed volunteering in the shop a couple of days a week, and that her friend had asked her to look out for the Hunger Games sequels for his daughter. I said how much I loved the shop and that I often used it to pick up replacements for books that I've owned but have lost or given away. It was a delightful little exchange and reminded me of everything I know and love about bookshops. Although I was the customer, the act of sorting out the order for her reminded me that one of the things I most loved about bookselling was that I felt useful.

Driving home, I pondered identity, the way we describe ourselves, what we can and can't choose. I used to be a sister, a smoker and a drinker, and I am no longer any of those things. Now I am a mother, a writer, a teacher and a mentor. And I will always be a reader.

On Sunday mornings I get up early – sometimes in the dark – and run down to my parents' boat for breakfast. My route takes me across the top of the graveyard where my granny is buried and where we put a plaque to remember Matty after scattering his ashes into the sea. I give them a wave as I run on to Swanpool, where smugglers used to bring in brandy and which always makes me think of *Jamaica Inn*, and then around the cliff, with the sea to my right and Pendennis Castle up ahead.

Dad always has a grapefruit ready for me. I am too impatient to prepare grapefruit so I never buy them myself. Dad is careful and methodical and has always separated out the segments with his special curved knife, and I eat it knowing that it is a mark of his love for me, that he will go to this effort. I always think of Stuart in *Talking It Over* who de-pips Gillian's grapefruit, is upset she doesn't notice, and who thinks, when she leaves him for his friend Oliver, that there is no way Oliver will be capable of that level of dedication. In the last chapter in *A History of the World in 10½ Chapters*, when the narrator wakes up in heaven, the first thing he eats is a perfect grapefruit.

Sometimes Matt comes on the run with me. I've realized lately that, just because I think it would have been brilliant to have a writer as a parent and have their writerly friends hanging around the house, this isn't necessarily how Matt feels. Quite simply, he doesn't like anything that takes me away, whether that is literal or metaphorical travelling. When he was much smaller, he would come up to me when I was thinking and knock against my forehead: 'Are you in there, Mummy? Where are you?' Recently, reading the acknowledgements in the latest Robert Galbraith novel, I saw that the author thanks her children and says that being the child of a writer is not an easy shift. I asked Matt about it that night: 'Is that true, do you think? Why?'

'Yes,' he said. 'We always think you love your books more than you love us.'

'I don't love anything more than I love you,' I said, and he gave me a little smile, as though he didn't quite believe me.

'I love you more than any book, you know,' I said.

'Do you?'

'Oh yes.'

'Then that's a lot,' he said, 'because you really love books.'

'I know,' I said. 'Imagine being the boy who is loved more than all the books that I've ever read. That's a lot of love.'

'I believe there is a theory,' says Mrs de Winter, as she thinks back to everything that happened at Manderley, 'that men and women emerge finer and stronger after suffering, and that to advance in this or any world we must endure ordeal by fire.' She goes on to say that sooner or later in everyone's life there will be a moment of trial, and that having come through her crisis, she has had enough of melodrama. I feel the same. I tremble for the world but try to enjoy the gentle rhythms of every-day life, and rather hope that the gods of story will leave me alone for a while.

Back in Snaith, when I was a girl, I longed for something to happen to me. Now, I rather hope that nothing does. I would like to potter about, hopefully putting more good than bad into the world and finding ways to be of service, but otherwise raising my child, cultivating my garden, and enjoying the company of my family and friends and the many magnificent, tattered volumes on my bookshelves. Which are still out of order, by the way. I can't fix on a satisfactory shelving method and my resolutions not to let piles of books teeter out of control never last.

Every book holds a memory. When you hold a book in your hand, you access not only the contents of that book but the fragments of the previous selves that you were when you read it. Looking ahead – tearing myself out of the past for a moment and looking into the future – I know that I will always be reading books and finding great comfort and joy between the pages. And maybe, when I am old or ill, when the font is too small, I will listen to them instead. Perhaps the voice I will hear when I am dying is Maya Angelou reading *I Know Why the Caged Bird Sings*, or maybe Matt or even one of his children might read to me. That would not be a bad way to go.

Until then, I can keep looking in wardrobes and know that no matter what happens to me, as long as I have breath in my body I will remember the joy of lying under a tree with a book in my parents' garden, the bliss of reading to my son, and the very many strangers I have met over the years in bookshops, libraries, festivals, prisons, and on planes and trains, and that those moments of human connection have happened on the bridge that books have built between me and the world I live in. We are all in the gutter, but books allow us to see the stars. And I know that whatever else may happen in my life, I will love talking to strangers about books. Once upon a time there was a little girl who loved books. She still does. She always will.

'There are no endings. If you think so you are deceived as to their nature. They are all beginnings. Here is one.'

Hilary Mantel, Bring Up the Bodies

Acknowledgements

This book was a long time in the writing because whenever my mood crashed I would doubt my own thesis – that life is worth living and that reading is an ally – and would struggle to carry on. Eventually I realized that these ups and downs were affirming my thesis as I followed the same pattern of getting depressed, retreating back into my old favourites and then feeling well enough to re-engage. Finally I worked out that this project, and possibly all my endeavours, could be summed up as: 'Life hurts; books help.'

The upside of it taking so long was that I got to have three wonderful editors, and I'm hugely grateful to Francesca Main, Kish Widyaratna and Gillian Fitzgerald-Kelly. Heartfelt thanks also to my agent and friend Jo Unwin and to Milly Reilly and Donna Greaves at JULA. It is a privilege to be in the care of such amazing women.

I wanted to thank all the writers with whom I have had stimulating backstage conversations about this book but it looked like an exercise in name-dropping so I will confine myself to saying 'You know who you are.' Huge thanks to booksellers, librarians and festival organizers for being the lifeblood in the connection between authors and readers. A special shout-out to my Cornish locals: Falmouth Library, the Falmouth Bookseller and the Waterstones in Truro.

Thanks to all at Arvon, Curtis Brown Creative, Falmouth University, the Koestler Trust, Spread the Word, Clean Prose and the National Centre for Writing for giving me opportunities to nurture writers. A cheery wave goes out to all my students and mentees: you light me up.

In the later stages of writing the book I had a blast presenting the *Bookseller* podcast. Thanks to Nigel Roby, Philip Jones, Tom Tivnan, Alice O'Keefe, Caroline Sanderson and Chris Thompson for making it so much fun, and to all our authors, especially Bernardine Evaristo who made time for us in the hectic aftermath of winning the Booker Prize. (And incidentally becoming the second Quick Reads author to win the Booker and the first to do it that way around.)

For all sorts of support I am indebted to Alison Belshaw, Roberta Boyce, Claire de Boursac, Sara Collins, Esther Connor, Jo Dawson, Kate Dimbleby, Janine Giovanni, Sali Hughes, Mia Kawada, Sophie Kirkham, Fiona Lockhart, Crystal Mahey-Morgan, Wyl Menmuir, Sanja Oakley, Julia Samuel, Nina Stibbe and Kit de Waal.

Thanks to John and Lizzie Waterhouse for giving me a home from home and to Alice and Annie for always making me feel so welcome.

I'm grateful to Isla Morrison for our lifelong friendship. When I sent her the bit I'd written about her she made me cry with this beautiful response: 'Where you found me/us glamorous and sophisticated I thought you were the luckiest girl in the world with the amount of unconditional love you were surrounded with at home from darling Mig and Kev. I don't think I minded quite as much as you think about you disappearing into books for the weekend, as I was so happy spending time with your parents and Matty! Being at your house on a Sunday afternoon watching *Bullseye* with a tray of tea and an overflowing plate of Wagon Wheels and Tunnock's Teacakes was a highlight of my week! Being a part of the family unit (even for a few days at a time) was a lifeline to normality for me at the time and I have never underestimated the long-lasting and positive effect it has had. I have nothing but happy memories full of love and laughter at my time with you all.'

Lastly, the home front. Thanks to my parents, Kevin and Miggy, for continuing to look after me and for injecting fun and larks into the cultivation of the garden. Long may it continue. I'm grateful to Ada Rentzenbrink and Paul and Marion Bowyer for their help and company. Thanks to my husband, Erwyn, for being a good sort and for learning to restrain himself from discussing the issues of the day with me until after I've done my daily shift at the writing coalface. Thanks to my son, Matt, for many fascinating conversations about books and stories and for being a constant source of support and delight.

Matt says it is unfair if I don't mention our pets so I'll finish with a nod to Arabella the cat and Reepicheep the lizard. And, if I'm doing animals, thanks also to Rainbow, Peggy and Fudge for graciously allowing me to hang out with their owners.

Much love also to you, dear reader. Writing anything feels like an opening gambit to me – the start of a conversation – and I am thrilled and honoured whenever anyone answers back. My books are like flat balloons waiting for a reader to come along and breathe life into them. Thank you for letting me take flight in your imagination. May you have all of the pineapple cubes.

Writing can be a lonely act but I am always both heartened and encouraged by the prospect of contact with my amazing publisher and the many talented and lovely people who work so hard to get books out into the world. I'm delighted to be able to list them all by name and role in the credits that follow.

Credits

Publisher, Macmillan Adult Books Jeremy Trevathan

Associate Publisher Francesca Main

Editor Gillian Fitzgerald-Kelly

Finance Director, Pan Macmillan Lara Borlenghi

Finance Director, Adult Publishing Jo Mower

Head of Contracts Clare Miller

Contracts Assistant Senel Enver

Audio Publishing Director Rebecca Lloyd

Associate Publisher Sophie Brewer

Managing Editor Laura Carr

Copy-editor Claire Gatzen

Desk Editor Chloe May

Art and Design Director James Annal

Jacket Designer Lucy Scholes

Studio Manager Lloyd Jones

Head of Adult Production Simon Rhodes

Senior Production Controller Charlotte Tonner

Production Controller Giacomo Russo

Text Design Manager Lindsay Nash

Communications Director, Picador Emma Bravo

Publicist Camilla Elworthy

Senior Communications Executive Gabriela Quattromini

The UK Sales Team

Trade Marketing Manager Ruth Brooks

International Director Jonathan Atkins

Head of International Sales, Picador Emily Scorer

Rights Director Jon Mitchell

Senior Rights Manager Anna Shora

Rights Executive Mairéad Loftus

Rights Assistant Aisling Brennan

Marketing and Communications Director Lee Dibble

Senior Metadata and Content Manager Eleanor Jones

Metadata Executive Marisa Davies

Digital Publishing Senior Executive Alex Ellis

Operations Manager Kerry Pretty

Operations Administrator Josh Craig